lonely planet

≡ Fast Talk

German

Guaranteed to get you talking

Contents

⇛ Special Features

Before You Go

It is possible to travel in Germany without speaking a word of German, but just a few phrases go a long way in making friends, inviting service with a smile, and ensuring a rich and rewarding travel experience – you could discover a hidden Berlin bar, find the best new fashion boutiques, or be able to buy last-minute tickets to the opera.

PRONUNCIATION TIPS

The sounds of German can almost all be found in English, and if you read our coloured pronunciation guides as if they were English you'll have no problems being understood. The stressed syllables are indicated with italics.

★ The few sounds that do differ from English include the ü (pronounced as the 'ee' in 'see' with rounded lips), plus kh (pronounced at the back of the throat, like in the Scottish *loch*) and r (also throaty, a bit like gargling).

★ Vowels are pronounced crisply and cleanly, with your mouth tenser than in English, eg *Tee* is pronounced tay, not *tay·ee*.

★ Note also that zh is pronounced as the 's' in 'pleasure'.

MUST-KNOW GRAMMAR

The structure of German holds no major surprises for English speakers since the two languages are quite closely related.

★ German has a formal and informal word for 'you' (*Sie* zee and *du* doo respectively). When talking to someone familiar or younger than you, use the informal *du* form.

4

Phrases in this book use the form that is appropriate to the situation. Where both forms can be used, they are indicated by pol and inf respectively.

★ German also distinguishes between masculine and feminine forms of words, eg *Freund/Freundin* froynt/*froyn·*din (friend), indicated in this book by m and f. German also has neuter nouns, indicated with n where required.

★ German words can have a number of different endings, depending on their role in the sentence (it's similar to some verbs in English, eg 'I do' vs 'he/she do**es**'). Travellers don't need to worry too much about this though – if you use the dictionary form of a word in all contexts, you'll still be understood.

SOUNDS FAMILIAR?

Numerous German words are already part of the English vocabulary – you're sure to recognise *kindergarten, kitsch, waltz, hamburger, poodle…*

Fast Talk German

Don't worry if you've never learnt German (*Deutsch* doytsh) before – it's all about confidence. You don't need to memorise endless grammatical details or long lists of vocabulary – you just need to start speaking. You have nothing to lose and everything to gain when the locals hear you making an effort. And remember that body language and a sense of humour have a role to play in every culture.

"you just need to start speaking"

Even if you use the very basics, such as greetings and civilities, your travel experience will be the better for it. Once you start, you'll be amazed how many prompts you'll get to help you build on those first words. You'll hear people speaking, pick up sounds and expressions from the locals, catch a word or two that you know from TV already, see something on a billboard – all these things help to build your understanding.

5. *Phrases to Learn Before You Go*

1. Do you accept credit cards?
Nehmen Sie Kreditkarten?
*nay·*men zee kre·*deet·*kar·ten

Cash payment is still common in Germany, so don't assume you'll be able to pay by credit card – it's best to enquire first.

2. Which beer would you recommend?
Welches Bier empfehlen Sie?
*vel·*khes beer emp·*fay·*len zee

Who better to ask for advice on beer than the Germans, whether at a beer garden, hall, cellar or on a brewery tour?

3. Can I get this without meat?
Kann ich das ohne Fleisch bekommen?
kan ikh das *aw·*ne flaish be·*ko·*men

In the land of *Wurst* and *Schnitzel* it may be difficult to find a variety of vegetarian meals, especially in smaller towns.

4. A (non)smoking table, please.
Einen (Nicht)Rauchertisch, bitte.
*ai·*nen (*nikht·*)*row·*kher·tish *bi·*te

Germany and Austria have only partial smoking bans, so you may want to choose where to sit in cafes, bars and restaurants.

5. Do you run original versions?
Spielen auch Originalversionen?
*shpee·*len owkh o·ri·gi·*nahl·*fer·zi·*aw·*nen

German cinemas usually run movies dubbed into German – look for a cinema that runs subtitled original versions.

10. Phrases to Sound Like a Local

Hey!	**Hey!**	*hei*
Great!	**Toll!**	*tol*
Cool!	**Spitze!**	*shpi·tse*
No problem.	**Kein Problem.**	*kain pro·blaym*
Sure.	**Klar!**	*klahr*
Maybe.	**Vielleicht.**	*fi·laikht*
No way!	**Auf keinen Fall!**	*owf kai·nen fal*
It's OK.	**Alles klar.**	*a·les klahr*
What a pity!	**Schade!**	*shah·de*
Doesn't matter.	**Macht nichts.**	*makht nikhts*

10. Phrases to Start a Sentence

BEFORE YOU GO

When's (the next flight)?	Wann ist (der nächste Flug)? van ist (dair *naykhs*·te flook)
Where's (the station)?	Wo ist (der Bahnhof)? vaw ist (dair *bahn*·hawf)
Where do I (pay)?	Wo muss ich (bezahlen)? vaw mus ikh (be·*tsah*·len)
Do you have (a map)?	Haben Sie (eine Karte)? *hah*·ben zee (*ai*·ne *kar*·te)
Is there (a toilet)?	Gibt es (eine Toilette)? gipt es (*ai*·ne to·a·*le*·te)
I'd like (a coffee).	Ich möchte (einen Kaffee). ikh *merkh*·te (*ai*·nen *ka*·fay)
I'd like (to hire a car).	Ich möchte (ein Auto mieten). ikh *merkh*·te (ain *ow*·to *mee*·ten)
Can I (enter)?	Darf ich (hereinkommen)? darf ikh (her·*ein*·ko·men)
Can you please (help me)?	Könnten Sie (mir helfen)? *kern*·ten zee (meer *hel*·fen)
Do I have to (change trains)?	Muss ich (umsteigen)? mus ikh (*um*·shtai·gen)

Chatting & Basics

≡ Fast Phrases

Hello./Goodbye.	Guten Tag./ Auf Wiedersehen. *goo*·ten tahk/ owf *vee*·der·zay·en
Please./Thank you.	Bitte./Danke. *bi*·te/*dang*·ke
Do you speak English?	Sprechen Sie Englisch? *shpre*·khen zee *eng*·lish

Essentials

Yes./No.	Ja./Nein. yah/nain
Please.	Bitte. *bi*·te
Thank you.	Danke. *dang*·ke
Thank you very much.	Vielen Dank. *fee*·len dangk
You're (very) welcome.	Bitte (sehr). *bi*·te (zair)
Excuse me./Sorry.	Entschuldigung. ent·*shul*·di·gung

Language Difficulties

CHATTING & BASICS

Do you speak English?	Sprechen Sie Englisch? pol *shpre*·khen zee *eng*·lish Sprichst du Englisch? inf shprikhst doo *eng*·lish
Does anyone speak English?	Spricht hier jemand Englisch? shprikht heer *yay*·mant *eng*·lish
Do you understand (me)?	Verstehen Sie (mich)? fer·*shtay*·en zee (mikh)
I (don't) understand.	Ich verstehe (nicht). ikh fer·*shtay*·e (nikht)
I speak a little German.	Ich spreche ein bisschen Deutsch. ikh *shpre*·khe ain *bis*·khen doytsh
What does ... mean?	Was bedeutet ...? vas be·*doy*·tet ...
How do you pronounce this?	Wie spricht man dieses Wort aus? vee shprikht man *dee*·zes vort ows
How do you write ...?	Wie schreibt man ...? vee shraipt man ...
Could you please repeat that?	Könnten Sie das bitte wiederholen? *kern*·ten zee das *bi*·te vee·der·*haw*·len
Could you please write it down?	Könnten Sie das bitte aufschreiben? *kern*·ten zee das *bi*·te owf·shrai·ben
Could you please speak more slowly?	Könnten Sie bitte langsamer sprechen? *kern*·ten zee *bi*·te lang·za·mer *shpre*·khen
✂ **Slowly, please!**	Langsamer, bitte! *lang*·za·mer *bi*·te

Greetings

Hello.	Guten Tag. *goo·ten tahk*
Hi.	Hallo. *ha·lo*
Good morning.	Guten Morgen. *goo·ten mor·gen*
Good evening.	Guten Abend. *goo·ten ah·bent*
Good night.	Gute Nacht. *goo·te nakt*
See you later.	Bis später. *bis shpay·ter*
Goodbye.	Auf Wiedersehen. *owf vee·der·zay·en*
How are you?	Wie geht es Ihnen? pol *vee gayt es ee·nen* Wie geht es dir? inf *vee gayt es deer*
Fine, thanks. And you?	Danke, gut. Und Ihnen? pol *dang·ke goot unt ee·nen* Danke, gut. Und dir? inf *dang·ke goot unt deer*

> **Fast Talk** **Greetings**
> The standard greeting (Hello) in German
> varies depending on the destination: while *Guten Tag*
> *goo·ten tahk* is commonly used in all of Germany, you'll
> also hear *Grüß Gott* grüs got in the south of the country,
> *Grüezi grü·e·tsi* in Switzerland, and *Servus zer·vus* in
> Austria.

Titles

Mr	Herr *her*
Mrs	Frau *frow*
Miss	Fräulein *froy·lain*

Introductions

What's your name?	Wie ist Ihr Name? pol *vee ist eer nah·me* Wie heißt du? inf *vee haist doo*
My name is ...	Mein Name ist ... pol *main nah·me ist ...* Ich heiße ... inf *ikh hai·se ...*
I'm pleased to meet you.	Angenehm. *an·ge·naym*
It's been great meeting you.	Es war schön, Sie kennen zu lernen. pol *es vahr shern zee ke·nen tsoo ler·nen* Es war schön, dich kennen zu lernen. inf *es vahr shern dikh ke·nen tsoo ler·nen*
I'd like to introduce you to ...	Darf ich Ihnen ... vorstellen? pol *darf ikh ee·nen ... fawr·shte·len* Darf ich dir ... vorstellen? inf *darf ikh dir ... fawr·shte·len*

This is ...	Das ist ... das ist ...	

PHRASE BUILDER

This is my ...	Das ist ...	das ist ...
child	mein Kind	main kint
colleague	mein Kollege **m**	main ko·*lay*·ge
	meine Kollegin **f**	*mai*·ne ko·*lay*·gin
friend	mein Freund **m**	main froynt
	meine Freundin **f**	*mai*·ne *froyn*·din
husband	mein Mann	main man
partner	mein Partner **m**	main *part*·ner
	meine Partnerin **f**	*mai*·ne *part*·ne·rin
wife	meine Frau	*mai*·ne frow

What's your...?	Wie ist Ihre ...? **pol** vee ist *ee*·re ... Wie ist deine ...? **inf** vee ist *dai*·ne ...	

PHRASE BUILDER

Here's my ...	Hier ist meine ...	heer ist *mai*·ne ...
address	Adresse	a·*dre*·se
email address	E-mail-Adresse	ee·mayl·a·dre·se
mobile number	Handynummer	*hen*·di·nu·mer
phone number	Telefonnummer	te·le·*fawn*·nu·mer

Personal Details

Where are you from?	Woher kommen Sie? pol
	vaw·hair *ko*·men zee
	Woher kommst du? inf
	vaw·hair komst doo

I'm from ...	Ich komme aus ...	ikh *ko*·me ows ...
Australia	Australien	ows·*trah*·li·en
Canada	Kanada	*ka*·na·da
England	England	*eng*·lant
New Zealand	Neuseeland	noy·*zay*·lant
the USA	den USA	dayn oo·es·*ah*

Are you married?	Sind Sie verheiratet? pol
	zint zee fer·*hai*·ra·tet
	Bist du verheiratet? inf
	bist doo fer·*hai*·ra·tet
I'm single.	Ich bin ledig.
	ikh bin *lay*·dikh
I'm married.	Ich bin verheiratet.
	ikh bin fer·*hai*·ra·tet
I'm separated.	Ich bin getrennt.
	ikh bin ge·*trent*

Age

How old are you?	Wie alt sind Sie? pol
	vee alt zint zee
	Wie alt bist du? inf
	vee alt bist doo
I'm ... years old.	Ich bin ... Jahre alt.
	ikh bin ... *yah*·re alt

How old is your son?	Wie alt ist Ihr Sohn? pol
	vee alt ist eer zawn
	Wie alt ist dein Sohn? inf
	vee alt ist dain zawn
How old is your daughter?	Wie alt ist Ihre Tochter? pol
	vee alt ist *ee*·re *tokh*·ter
	Wie alt ist deine Tochter? inf
	vee alt ist *dai*·ne *tokh*·ter
He/She is ... years old.	Er/Sie ist ... Jahre alt.
	air/zee ist ... *yah*·re alt

Occupations & Study

What's your occupation?	Als was arbeiten Sie? pol
	als vas *ar*·bai·ten zee
	Als was arbeitest du? inf
	als vas *ar*·bai·test doo
I work in (IT).	Ich arbeite in (der IT-Branche).
	ikh *ar*·bai·te in (dair ai·*tee*·brang·she)
I work in (sales).	Ich arbeite im (Verkauf).
	ikh *ar*·bai·te im (fer·*kowf*)

PHRASE BUILDER

I'm (a) ...	Ich bin ...	ikh bin ...
retired	ein Rentner m	ain *rent*·ner
	eine Rentnerin f	*ain*·e *rent*·ne·rin
self-employed	selbstständig	zelpst·shten·dikh
student	ein Student m	ain shtu·*dent*
	eine Studentin f	*ain*·e shtu·*den*·tin
unemployed	arbeitslos	*ar*·baits·laws

What are you studying?	Was studieren Sie? pol
	vas shtu·*dee*·ren zee
	Was studierst du? inf
	vas shtu·*deerst* doo
I'm studying engineering.	Ich studiere
	Ingenieurwesen.
	ikh shtu·*dee*·re
	in·zhe·*nyer*·vay·zen
I'm studying German.	Ich studiere Deutsch.
	ikh shtu·*dee*·re doytsh

Interests

What do you do in your spare time?	Was machen Sie in Ihrer Freizeit? pol
	vas *ma*·khen zee in *ee*·rer *frai*·tsait
	Was machst du in deiner Freizeit? inf
	vas makhst doo in *dai*·ner *frai*·tsait
Do you like (art)?	Mögen Sie (Kunst)? pol
	mer·gen zee (kunst)
	Magst du (Kunst)? inf
	mahkst doo (kunst)
Do you like (sport)?	Mögen Sie (Sport)? pol
	mer·gen zee (shport)
	Magst du (Sport)? inf
	mahkst doo (shport)
I like (music).	Ich mag (Musik).
	ikh mahk (mu·*zeek*)
I don't like (movies).	Ich mag keine (Filme).
	ikh mahk *kai*·ne (*fil*·me)
I like (cooking).	Ich (koche) gern.
	ikh (*ko*·khe) gern

| I don't like (hiking). | Ich (wandere) nicht gern. |
| | ikh (*van*·de·re) nikht gern |

Feelings

Are you ...?	Sind Sie ...? pol
	zint zee ...
	Bist du ...? inf
	bist doo ...

PHRASE BUILDER		
I'm (not) ...	Ich bin (nicht) ...	ikh bin (nikht) ...
happy	glücklich	*glük*·likh
in a hurry	in Eile	in *ai*·le
sad	traurig	*trow*·rikh
tired	müde	*mü*·de

Are you (hungry)?	Haben Sie (Hunger)? pol
	hah·ben zee (*hung*·er)
	Hast du (Hunger)? inf
	hast doo (*hung*·er)
I'm not (thirsty).	Ich habe kein (Durst).
	ikh *hah*·be kain (durst)
Are you (hot)?	Ist Ihnen (heiß)? pol
	ist *ee*·nen (hais)
	Ist dir (heiß)? inf
	ist deer (hais)
I'm not (cold).	Mir ist nicht (kalt).
	meer ist nikht (kalt)
I feel very lucky.	Ich schätze mich sehr glücklich.
	ikh *she*·tse mikh zair *glük*·likh
I'm terribly sorry.	Es tut mir furchtbar Leid.
	es toot meer *furkht*·bahr lait

Numbers

1	eins	ains
2	zwei	tsvai
3	drei	drai
4	vier	feer
5	fünf	fünf
6	sechs	zeks
7	sieben	*zee*·ben
8	acht	akht
9	neun	noyn
10	zehn	tsayn
11	elf	elf
12	zwölf	tsverlf
13	dreizehn	*drai*·tsayn
14	vierzehn	*feer*·tsayn
17	siebzehn	*zeep*·tsayn
20	zwanzig	*tsvan*·tsikh
21	einundzwanzig	*ain*·unt·tsvan·tsikh
22	zweiundzwanzig	*tsvai*·unt·tsvan·tsikh
30	dreißig	*drai*·tsikh
40	vierzig	*feer*·tsikh
50	fünfzig	*fünf*·tsikh

Fast Talk — Telling the Time

The 24-hour clock is commonly used when telling the time in German. To denote the time between noon and midnight, use *nachmittags* nahkh·mi·tahks for times between noon and 6pm, and *abends* ah·bents for times from 6pm to midnight.

60	sechzig	*zekh*·tsikh
70	siebzig	*zeep*·tsikh
80	achtzig	*akht*·tsikh
90	neunzig	*noyn*·tsikh
100	hundert	*hun*·dert
1000	tausend	*tow*·sent
1,000,000	eine Million	*ai*·ne mil·*yawn*

Time

What time is it?	Wie spät ist es? vee shpayt ist es
It's (2.12pm).	Es ist (14:12). es ist (*feer*·tsayn oor tsverlf)
It's (10) o'clock.	Es ist (zehn) Uhr. es ist (tsayn) oor
Quarter past (one).	Viertel nach (eins). *fir*·tel nahkh (ains)
Half past one.	Halb zwei. (lit: half two) halp tsvai
Twenty to (one).	Zwanzig vor (eins). *tsvan*·tsikh fawr (ains)
At what time?	Um wie viel Uhr? um vee feel oor
At ...	Um ... um ...
in the morning	vormittags *fawr*·mi·tahks
in the afternoon	nachmittags *nahkh*·mi·tahks
in the evening	abends *ah*·bents

19

Fast Talk Starting Off

When starting to speak another language, your biggest hurdle is saying aloud what may seem to be just a bunch of sounds. The best way to do this is to memorise a few key words, like 'hello', 'thank you' and 'how much?', plus at least one phrase that's not essential, eg 'how are you', 'see you later' or 'it's very cold/hot' (people love to talk about the weather!). This will enable you to make contact with the locals, and when you get a reply and a smile, it'll also boost your confidence.

Days

Monday	Montag m	*mawn*·tahk
Tuesday	Dienstag m	*deens*·tahk
Wednesday	Mittwoch m	*mit*·vokh
Thursday	Donnerstag m	*do*·ners·tahk
Friday	Freitag m	*frai*·tahk
Saturday	Samstag m	*zams*·tahk
Sunday	Sonntag m	*zon*·tahk

Months

January	Januar m	*yan*·u·ahr
February	Februar m	*fay*·bru·ahr
March	März m	merts
April	April m	a·*pril*
May	Mai m	mai
June	Juni m	*yoo*·ni

July	Juli m	*yoo*·li
August	August m	ow·*gust*
September	September m	zep·*tem*·ber
October	Oktober m	ok·*taw*·ber
November	November m	no·*vem*·ber
December	Dezember m	de·*tsem*·ber

Dates

What date?	Welches Datum? *vel*·khes *dah*·tum
What date is it today?	Der Wievielte ist heute? dair *vee*·feel·te ist *hoy*·te
It's (18 October) today.	Heute ist (der 18. Oktober). *hoy*·te ist (dair *akh*·tsayn·te ok·*taw*·ber)
yesterday morning	gestern Morgen *ges*·tern *mor*·gen
tomorrow morning	morgen früh *mor*·gen frü
yesterday afternoon	gestern Nachmittag *ges*·tern *nahkh*·mi·tahk
tomorrow afternoon	morgen Nachmittag *mor*·gen *nahkh*·mi·tahk
yesterday evening	gestern Abend *ges*·tern *ah*·bent
tomorrow evening	morgen Abend *mor*·gen *ah*·bent
last week	letzte Woche *lets*·te *vo*·khe
next week	nächste Woche *naykhs*·te *vo*·khe

last month	letzten Monat *lets*·ten *maw*·nat
next month	nächsten Monat *naykhs*·ten *maw*·nat
last year	letztes Jahr *lets*·tes yahr
next year	nächstes Jahr *naykhs*·tes yahr

Weather

What's the weather like?	Wie ist das Wetter? vee ist das *ve*·ter
What's the weather forecast?	Wie ist der Wetterbericht? vee ist dair *ve*·ter·be·rikht
It's raining.	Es regnet. es *reg*·net
It's snowing.	Es schneit. es shnait

PHRASE BUILDER

It's ...	Es ist ...	es ist ...
cold	kalt	kalt
hot	heiß	hais
sunny	sonnig	*zo*·nikh
windy	windig	*vin*·dikh

Directions

| Where's (a bank)? | Wo ist (eine Bank)?
vaw ist (*ai*·ne bangk) |

What's the address?	Wie ist die Adresse? *vee ist dee a·dre·se*
Could you please write it down?	Könnten Sie das bitte aufschreiben? *kern·ten zee das bi·te owf·shrai·ben*
Can you show me (on the map)?	Können Sie es mir (auf der Karte) zeigen? *ker·nen zee es meer (owf dair kar·te) tsai·gen*
How far is it?	Wie weit ist es? *vee vait ist es*
Turn at the corner.	Biegen Sie an der Ecke ab. *bee·gen zee an dair e·ke ap*
Turn at the traffic lights.	Biegen Sie bei der Ampel ab. *bee·gen zee bai dair am·pel ap*
Turn left.	Biegen Sie links ab. *bee·gen zee lingks ap*
Turn right.	Biegen Sie rechts ab. *bee·gen zee rekhts ap*
behind ...	hinter ... *hin·ter ...*
in front of ...	vor ... *fawr ...*
next to ...	neben ... *nay·ben ...*
opposite ...	gegenüber ... *gay·gen·ü·ber ...*
straight ahead	geradeaus *ge·rah·de·ows*

Airport & Transport

≡ Fast Phrases

When's the next (bus)?	Wann fährt der nächste (Bus)? van fairt dair *naykhs*·te (bus)
Does this (train) stop at ...?	Hält dieser (Zug) in ...? helt *dee*·zer (tsook) in ...
One ticket to ..., please.	Eine Fahrkarte nach ..., bitte. *ai*·ne *fahr*·kar·te nahkh ... *bi*·te

At the Airport

I'm here on business.	Ich bin hier auf Geschäftsreise. ikh bin heer owf ge·*shefts*·rai·ze
I'm here on holiday.	Ich bin hier im Urlaub. ikh bin heer im *oor*·lowp
I'm here for (three) days.	Ich bin hier für (drei) Tage. ikh bin heer für (drai) *tah*·ge
I'm here for (two) weeks.	Ich bin hier für (zwei) Wochen. ikh bin heer für (tsvai) *vo*·khen

I'm in transit.	Ich bin hier auf der Durchreise.
	ikh bin heer owf dair *durkh*·rai·ze
I'm going to (Salzburg).	Ich gehe nach (Salzburg).
	ikh *gay*·e nahkh (*zalts*·burg)
I have nothing to declare.	Ich habe nichts zu verzollen.
	ikh *hah*·be nikhts tsoo fer·*tso*·len
I have something to declare.	Ich habe etwas zu verzollen.
	ikh *hah*·be *et*·vas tsoo fer·*tso*·len

Getting Around

PHRASE BUILDER

At what time does the ... leave?	Wann fährt ... ab?	van fairt ... ap
boat	das Boot	das bawt
bus	der Bus	dair bus
plane	das Flugzeug	das *flook*·tsoyk
train	der Zug	dair tsook

When's the first bus?	Wann fährt der erste Bus?
	van fairt dair *ers*·te bus
When's the last bus?	Wann fährt der letzte Bus?
	van fairt dair *lets*·te bus
When's the next bus?	Wann fährt der nächste Bus?
	van fairt dair *naykhs*·te bus
How long does the trip take?	Wie lange dauert die Fahrt?
	vee *lang*·e *dow*·ert dee fahrt

Is it a direct route?	Ist es eine direkte Verbindung?
	ist es *ai*·ne di·*rek*·te fer·*bin*·dung
That's my seat.	Dieses ist mein Platz.
	dee·zes ist main plats
Is this seat free?	Ist dieser Platz frei?
	ist *dee*·zer plats frai
✂ **Is it free?**	Ist hier frei?
	ist heer frai

Buying Tickets

Where can I buy a ticket?	Wo kann ich eine Fahrkarte kaufen?
	vaw kan ikh *ai*·ne *fahr*·kar·te *kow*·fen
Do I need to book?	Muss ich einen Platz reservieren lassen?
	mus ikh *ai*·nen plats re·zer·*vee*·ren *la*·sen
What time do I have to check in?	Wann muss ich einchecken?
	van mus ikh *ain*·che·ken

Fast Talk Asking Questions

The easiest way of forming 'yes/no' questions is to add *nicht wahr* nikht var (lit: not true) to the end of a statement, similar to 'isn't it?' in English.

The question words for more specific questions go at the start of the sentence: *wie* vee (how), *was* vas (what), *wann* van (when), *wo* vaw (where), *wer* vair (who) or *warum* va·*rum* (why).

One ... ticket (to Berlin), please.	Eine ... (nach Berlin), bitte.	*ai*·ne ... (nahkh ber·*leen*) *bi*·te
1st-class	Fahrkarte erster Klasse	*fahr*·kar·te *ers*·ter *kla*·se
2nd-class	Fahrkarte zweiter Klasse	*fahr*·kar·te *tsvai*·ter *kla*·se
child's	Kinderfahrkarte	*kin*·der·fahr·kar·te
one-way	einfache Fahrkarte	*ain*·fa·khe *fahr*·kar·te
return	Rückfahrkarte	*rük*·fahr·kar·te
student's	Studenten-fahrkarte	shtu·*den*·ten·fahr·kar·te

I'd like an aisle seat.	Ich hätte gern einen Platz am Gang. ikh *he*·te gern *ai*·nen plats am gang
I'd like a window seat.	Ich hätte gern einen Fensterplatz. ikh *he*·te gern *ai*·nen *fens*·ter·plats
I'd like a (non)smoking seat.	Ich hätte gern einen (Nicht)Raucherplatz. ikh *he*·te gern *ai*·nen (*nikht*·)row·kher·plats
day ticket	Tageskarte f *tah*·ges·kar·te
weekly ticket	Wochenkarte f *vo*·khen·kar·te
ticket for multiple trips	Mehrfachfahrkarte f *mair*·fakh·fahr·kar·te

Luggage

My luggage has been damaged.	Mein Gepäck ist beschädigt. main ge·*pek* ist be·*shay*·dikht
My luggage has been stolen.	Mein Gepäck ist gestohlen worden. main ge·*pek* ist ge·*shtaw*·len *vor*·den
My luggage has been lost.	Mein Gepäck ist verloren gegangen. main ge·*pek* ist fer·*law*·ren ge·*gang*·en
I'd like a luggage locker.	Ich hätte gern ein Gepäckschließfach. ikh *he*·te gern ain ge·*pek*·shlees·fakh
Can I have some coins/ tokens?	Können Sie mir ein paar Münzen/Wertmarken geben? *ker*·nen zee meer ain pahr *mün*·tsen/*vert*·mar·ken *gay*·ben

Bus & Train

Where's the bus stop?	Wo ist die Bushaltestelle? vo ist dee *bus*·hal·te·shte·le
Which bus goes to ...?	Welcher Bus fährt nach ...? *vel*·kher bus fairt nakh ...
Is this the bus to ...?	Fährt dieser Bus nach ...? fairt *dee*·zer bus nakh ...
What station is this?	Welcher Bahnhof ist das? *vel*·kher *bahn*·hawf ist das
What's the next stop?	Welches ist der nächste Halt? *vel*·khes ist dair *naykh*·ste halt

What's the next station?	Welches ist der nächste Bahnhof? *vel*·khes ist dair *naykhs*·te *bahn*·hawf
Does this train stop at ...?	Hält dieser Zug in ...? helt *dee*·zer tsook in ...
Do I need to change trains?	Muss ich umsteigen? mus ikh *um*·shtai·gen
Can you tell me when we get to ...?	Könnten Sie mir bitte sagen, wann wir in ... ankommen? *kern*·ten zee meer *bi*·te *zah*·gen van veer in ... *an*·ko·men
I want to get off (at Alexanderplatz).	Ich möchte (am Alexanderplatz) aussteigen. ikh *merkh*·te (am a·lek·*san*·der·plats) *ows*·shtai·gen
I want to get off here.	Ich möchte hier aussteigen. ikh *merkh*·te heer *ows*·shtai·gen

Taxi

Where's the taxi stand?	Wo ist der Taxenstand? vaw ist dair *tak*·sen·shtant
I'd like a taxi at (9am).	Ich hätte gern ein Taxi für (neun Uhr). ikh *he*·te gern ain *tak*·si für (noyn oor)
Are you available?	Sind Sie frei? zint zee frai
How much is it to ...?	Was kostet es bis ...? vas *kos*·tet es bis ...

Please put the meter on.	Schalten Sie bitte den Taxameter ein. *shal*·ten zee *bi*·te dayn tak·sa·*may*·ter ain
Please take me to (this address).	Bitte bringen Sie mich zu (dieser Adresse). *bi*·te *bring*·en zee mikh tsoo (*dee*·zer a·*dre*·se)
✂ **To...**	Zu... tsoo
Please slow down.	Fahren Sie bitte langsamer. *fah*·ren zee *bi*·te *lang*·za·mer
Please wait here.	Bitte warten Sie hier. *bi*·te *var*·ten zee heer
Stop at the corner.	Halten Sie an der Ecke. *hal*·ten zee an dair *e*·ke
Stop here.	Halten Sie hier. *hal*·ten zee heer

Car & Motorbike

I'd like to hire a car.	Ich möchte ein Auto mieten. ikh *merkh*·te ain *ow*·to *mee*·ten
I'd like to hire a motorbike.	Ich möchte ein Motorrad mieten. ikh *merkh*·te ain *maw*·tor·raht *mee*·ten
How much is it per day?	Wie viel kostet es pro Tag? vee feel *kos*·tet es praw tahk
How much is it per week?	Wie viel kostet es pro Woche? vee feel *kos*·tet es praw *vo*·khe
Does this road go to ...?	Führt diese Straße nach ...? fürt *dee*·ze *shtrah*·se nahkh ...

Fast Talk **German Words**

Don't be intimidated by the length of some German words. Unlike English, which often uses a number of separate words to express a single notion, German tends to join words together. After a while you'll start to recognise parts of words and find it easy to understand longer words. For example, *haupt* howpt means 'main', so *Hauptpost* howpt·post means 'main post office', and *Hauptstadt* howpt·shtat is 'main city', ie 'capital'. Also keep in mind that nouns start with a capital letter in German, making it very easy to recognise them.

(How long) Can I park here?	(Wie lange) Kann ich hier parken? (vee *lang*·e) kan ikh heer *par*·ken
Where's a petrol station?	Wo ist eine Tankstelle? vaw ist *ai*·ne *tangk*·shte·le

Cycling

Where can I hire a bicycle?	Wo kann ich ein Fahrrad mieten? vaw kan ikh ain fahr·raht mee·ten
Are there cycling paths?	Gibt es Fahrradwege? geept es *fahr*·raht·vay·ge
Is there bicycle parking?	Gibt es Fahrrad-Parkplätze? geept es *fahr*·raht·park·ple·tse

31

Accommodation

⇒ Fast Phrases

I have a reservation.	Ich habe eine Reservierung.
	ikh *hah*·be *ai*·ne re·zer·*vee*·rung
When/Where is breakfast served?	Wann/Wo gibt es Frühstück?
	van/vaw gipt es *frü*·shtük
What time is checkout?	Wann muss ich auschecken?
	van mus ikh *ows*·che·ken

Finding Accommodation

PHRASE BUILDER

Where's a ...?	Wo ist ...?	vaw ist ...
bed and breakfast	eine Pension	*ai*·ne pahng·*zyawn*
camping ground	ein Camping-platz	ain *kem*·ping·plats
guesthouse	eine Pension	*ai*·ne pahng·*zyawn*
hotel	ein Hotel	ain ho·*tel*
youth hostel	eine Jugend-herberge	*ai*·ne *yoo*·gent·her·ber·ge

Booking & Checking In

I have a reservation.	Ich habe eine Reservierung.
	ikh *hah*·be *ai*·ne
	re·zer·*vee*·rung
Do you have a single room?	Haben Sie ein Einzelzimmer?
	hah·ben zee ain
	ain·tsel·tsi·mer
Do you have a double room?	Haben Sie ein Doppelzimmer mit einem Doppelbett?
	hah·ben zee ain *do*·pel·tsi·mer
	mit *ai*·nem *do*·pel·bet
Do you have a twin room?	Haben Sie ein Doppelzimmer mit zwei Einzelbetten?
	hah·ben zee ain *do*·pel·tsi·mer
	mit tsvai ain·tsel·*be*·ten
✄ **Are there rooms?**	Gibt es freie Zimmer?
	gipt es *fra*·ye *tsi*·mer
How much is it per night?	Wie viel kostet es pro Nacht?
	vee feel *kos*·tet es praw nakht
How much is it per person?	Wie viel kostet es pro Person?
	vee feel *kos*·tet es praw
	per·*zawn*
How much is it per week?	Wie viel kostet es pro Woche?
	vee feel *kos*·tet es praw *vo*·khe
For (three) nights.	Für (drei) Nächte.
	für (drai) *nekh*·te
From (July 2) to (July 6).	Vom (2. Juli) bis zum (6. Juli).
	vom (*tsvai*·ten *yoo*·li) bis
	tsum (*zeks*·ten *yoo*·li)

Can I see it?	Kann ich es sehen?
	kan ikh es *zay*·en
Is breakfast included?	Ist das Frühstück inklusive?
	ist das *frü*·shtük in·kloo·*zee*·ve
It's fine, I'll take it.	Es ist gut, ich nehme es.
	es ist goot ikh *nay*·me es
Do I need to pay upfront?	Muss ich im Voraus bezahlen?
	mus ikh im *faw*·rows be·*tsah*·len

Requests & Questions

When/Where is breakfast served?	Wann/Wo gibt es Frühstück?
	van/vaw gipt es *frü*·shtük
Please wake me at (seven).	Bitte wecken Sie mich um (sieben) Uhr.
	bi·te *ve*·ken zee mikh um (*zee*·ben) oor
Can I have my key, please?	Könnte ich bitte meinen Schlüssel haben?
	kern·te ikh *bi*·te *mai*·nen *shlü*·sel *hah*·ben
Can I use the kitchen?	Kann ich die Küche benutzen?
	kan ikh dee *kü*·khe be·*nu*·tsen
Can I use the telephone?	Kann ich das Telefon benutzen?
	kan ikh das te·le·*fawn* be·*nu*·tsen

Local Knowledge   Hotels

Can you recommend somewhere cheap?	Können Sie etwas Billiges empfehlen? *ker·nen zee et·vas bi·li·ges emp·fay·len*
Can you recommend somewhere nearby?	Können Sie etwas in der Nähe empfehlen? *ker·nen zee et·vas in dair nay·e emp·fay·len*
Can you recommend somewhere romantic?	Können Sie etwas Romantisches empfehlen? *ker·nen zee et·vas ro·man·ti·shes emp·fay·len*

Can I use the internet?	Kann ich das Internet benutzen? *kan ikh das in·ter·net be·nu·tsen*
Do you have an elevator?	Haben Sie einen Aufzug? *hah·ben zee ai·nen owf·tsook*
Do you have a laundry service?	Haben Sie einen Wäscheservice? *hah·ben zee ai·nen ve·she·ser·vis*
Do you have a safe?	Haben Sie einen Safe? *hah·ben zee ai·nen sayf*
Do you change money here?	Wechseln Sie hier Geld? *vek·seln zee heer gelt*
Do you arrange tours here?	Arrangieren Sie hier Touren? *a·rang·zhee·ren zee heer too·ren*

Fast Talk **Using Patterns**

Look out for patterns of words or phrases that stay the same, even when the situation changes, eg 'Do you have ...?' or 'I'd like to ...' (see p8). If you can recognise these patterns, you're already halfway to creating a full phrase. The dictionary will help you put other words together with these patterns to convey your meaning – even if it's not completely grammatically correct in all contexts, the dictionary form will always be understood.

Complaints

There's no hot water.	Es gibt kein warmes Wasser. es geept kain *var*·mes *va*·ser

PHRASE BUILDER

The ... doesn't work.	... funktioniert nicht.	... fungk·tsyaw·*neert* nikht
air-conditioning	Die Klimaanlage	dee *klee*·ma·an·lah·ge
heater	Das Heizgerät	das *haits*·ge·rayt
toilet	Die Toilette	dee to·a·*le*·te
window	Das Fenster	das *fens*·ter

It's too dark.	Es ist zu dunkel. es ist tsoo *dung*·kel
It's too noisy.	Es ist zu laut. es ist tsoo lowt
It's too small.	Es ist zu klein. es ist tsoo klain

PHRASE BUILDER

Can I get another ...?	Kann ich noch ... bekommen?	kan ikh nokh ... be·ko·men
blanket	eine Decke	ai·ne de·ke
pillow	ein Kopfkissen	ain kopf·ki·sen
sheet	ein Bettlaken	ain bet·lah·ken
towel	ein Handtuch	ain hant·tookh

Checking Out

What time is checkout?	Wann muss ich auschecken?	van mus ikh ows·che·ken
Can I leave my bags here until (tonight)?	Kann ich meine Taschen bis (heute Abend) hier lassen? kan ikh mai·ne ta·shen bis (hoy·te ah·bent) heer la·sen	
Can I have my deposit, please?	Könnte ich bitte meine Anzahlung haben? kern·te ikh bi·te mai·ne an·tsah·lung hah·ben	
Can I have my valuables, please?	Könnte ich bitte meine Wertsachen haben? kern·te ikh bi·te mai·ne vert·za·khen hah·ben	
I had a great stay, thank you.	Es hat mir hier sehr gut gefallen. es hat meer heer zair goot ge·fa·len	

Eating & Drinking

Fast Phrases

Can I see the menu, please?	Kann ich die Speisekarte sehen, bitte? kan ikh dee *shpai·ze·kar·te zay·*en *bi·*te
I'd like (a beer).	Ich möchte (ein Bier). ikh *merkh·*te (ain beer)
Please bring the bill.	Bitte bringen Sie die Rechnung. *bi·*te *bring·*en zee dee *rekh·*nung

Meals

breakfast	Frühstück n *frü·*shtük
lunch	Mittagessen n *mi·*tahk·e·sen
dinner	Abendessen n *ah·*bent·e·sen
eat	essen *e·*sen
drink	trinken *tring·*ken

Finding a Place to Eat

Can you recommend a bar/pub?	Können Sie eine Kneipe empfehlen? *ker·nen zee ai·ne knai·pe emp·fay·len*
Can you recommend a coffee bar?	Können Sie eine Espressobar empfehlen? *ker·nen zee ai·ne es·pre·so·bahr emp·fay·len*
Can you recommend a restaurant?	Können Sie ein Restaurant empfehlen? *ker·nen zee ain res·to·rang emp·fay·len*
I'd like to reserve a table for (eight) o'clock.	Ich möchte einen Tisch für (acht) Uhr reservieren. *ikh merkh·te ai·nen tish für (akht) oor re·zer·vee·ren*
I'd like to reserve a table for (two) people.	Ich möchte einen Tisch für (zwei) Personen reservieren. *ikh merkh·te ai·nen tish für (tsvai) per·zaw·nen re·zer·vee·ren*
For two, please.	Für zwei, bitte. *für tsvai bi·te*
I'd like a (non)smoking table, please.	Ich hätte gern einen (Nicht) Rauchertisch, bitte. *ikh he·te gern ai·nen (nikht·) row·kher·tish bi·te*
Are you still serving food?	Gibt es noch etwas zu essen? *gipt es nokh et·vas tsoo e·sen*
How long is the wait?	Wie lange muss man warten? *vee lang·e mus man var·ten*

Ordering & Paying

I'd like the menu, please.	Ich hätte gern die Speisekarte, bitte. ikh *he*·te gern dee *shpai*·ze·kar·te *bi*·te
✂ Menu, please.	Die Karte, bitte. dee *kar*·te *bi*·te
What would you recommend?	Was empfehlen Sie? vas emp·*fay*·len zee
I'd like a local speciality.	Ich möchte etwas Typisches aus der Region. ikh *merkh*·te *et*·vas *tü*·pi·shes ows dair re·*gyawn*
I'd like that dish.	Ich möchte dieses Gericht. ikh *merkh*·te *dee*·zes ge·*rikht*

Local Knowledge — Restaurants

Where would you go for a cheap meal?	Wo kann man hingehen, um etwas Billiges zu essen? vaw kan man *hin*·gay·en um *et*·vas *bi*·li·ges tsoo e·sen
Where would you go for local specialities?	Wo kann man hingehen, um örtliche Spezialitäten zu essen? vaw kan man *hin*·gay·en um *ert*·li·khe shpe·tsya·li·*tay*·ten tsoo e·sen
Where would you go for a celebration?	Wo kann man hingehen, um etwas zu feiern? vaw kan man *hin*·gay·en um *et*·vas tsoo *fai*·ern

I'd like the drink list, please.	Ich hätte gern die Getränkekarte, bitte. ikh *he*·te gern dee ge·*treng*·ke·kar·te *bi*·te
We're just having drinks.	Wir möchten nur etwas trinken. veer *merkh*·ten noor *et*·vas *tring*·ken
Just drinks.	Nur Getränke. noor ge·*treng*·ke

PHRASE BUILDER

I'd like it ...	Ich hätte es gern ...	ikh *he*·te es gern ...
medium	halb durch	halp durkh
rare	englisch	*eng*·lish
steamed	gedämpft	ge·*dempft*
well-done	gut durchgebraten	goot *durkh*·ge·brah·ten
with (the dressing on the side)	mit (dem Dressing daneben)	mit (daym *dre*·sing da·*nay*·ben)
without ...	ohne ...	*aw*·ne ...

Please bring (a glass).	Bitte bringen Sie (ein Glas). *bi*·te *bring*·en zee (ain glahs)
I didn't order this.	Das habe ich nicht bestellt. das *hah*·be ikh nikht be·*shtelt*
This is (too) cold.	Das ist (zu) kalt. das ist (tsoo) kalt
That was delicious!	Das hat hervorragend geschmeckt! das hat her·*fawr*·rah·gent ge·*shmekt*

41

Practising German

If you want to practise your language skills, try the waiters at a restaurant. Find your feet with straight-forward phrases such as asking for a table and ordering a drink, then initiate a conversation by asking for menu recommendations or asking how a dish is cooked. And as you'll often know food terms even before you've 'officially' learnt a word of the language, you're already halfway to understanding the response.

Please bring the bill.		Bitte bringen Sie die Rechnung.
		*bi·*te *bring·*en zee dee *rekh·*nung
✂	**Bill, please.**	Die Rechnung, bitte.
		dee *rekh·*nung *bi·*te
There's a mistake in the bill.		Da ist ein Fehler in der Rechnung.
		dah ist ain *fay·*ler in dair *rekh·*nung

Special Diets & Allergies

Is there a vegetarian restaurant near here?	Gibt es ein vegetarisches Restaurant hier in der Nähe?
	gipt es ain ve·ge·*tah·*ri·shes res·to·*rang* heer in dair *nay·*e
Do you have vegetarian food?	Haben Sie vegetarisches Essen?
	*hah·*ben zee ve·ge·*tah·*ri·shes *e·*sen
I'm a vegan.	Ich bin Veganer/Veganerin. m/f
	ikh bin ve·*gah·*ner/ve·*gah·*ne·rin

I'm a vegetarian.	Ich bin Vegetarier/ Vegetarierin. m/f
	ikh bin ve·ge·*tah*·ri·er/ ve·ge·*tah*·ri·e·rin
I don't eat (meat).	Ich esse kein (Fleisch).
	ikh *e*·se kain (flaish)
Could you prepare a meal without (butter)?	Können Sie ein Gericht ohne (Butter) zubereiten?
	ker·nen zee ain ge·*rikht aw*·ne (*bu*·ter) *tsoo*·be·rai·ten

---

PHRASE BUILDER

I'm allergic to ...	Ich bin allergisch gegen ...	ikh bin a·*lair*·gish *gay*·gen ...
dairy produce	Milchprodukte	*milkh*·pro·duk·te
eggs	Eier	*ai*·er
fish	Fisch	fish
gluten	Gluten	*gloo*·ten
nuts	Nüsse	*nü*·se
seafood	Meeresfrüchte	*mair*·res·frükh·te

Nonalcoholic Drinks

coffee (without sugar)	Kaffee (ohne Zucker) m
	ka·fay (*aw*·ne *tsu*·ker)
orange juice	Orangensaft m
	o·*rang*·zhen·zaft
soft drink	Softdrink m
	soft·dringk
tea (with milk)	Tee (mit Milch) m
	tay (mit milkh)
(mineral) water	(Mineral)Wasser n
	(mi·ne·*rahl*·)va·ser

Alcoholic Drinks

a shot of (gin)	einen (Gin) *ai*·nen (dzhin)
a bottle of beer	eine Flasche Bier *ai*·ne *fla*·she beer
a glass of beer	ein Glas Bier ain glahs beer
a pint of beer	ein halbes Bier ain *halb*·es beer

PHRASE BUILDER

a glass of ... wine	ein Glas ...	ain glahs ...
dessert	Dessertwein	de·*sair*·vain
red	Rotwein	*rawt*·vain
sparkling	Sekt	zekt
white	Weißwein	*vais*·vain

In the Bar

I'll buy you a drink.	Ich gebe Ihnen einen aus. pol ikh *gay*·be *ee*·nen *ai*·nen ows Ich gebe dir einen aus. inf ikh *gay*·be deer *ai*·nen ows
What would you like?	Was möchten Sie? pol vas *merkh*·ten zee Was möchtest du? inf vas *merkh*·test doo
I'll have ...	Ich hätte gern ... ikh *he*·te gern ...
Same again, please.	Dasselbe nochmal, bitte. das·*zel*·be nokh·*mahl* bi·te

It's my round.	Diese Runde geht auf mich.
	dee·ze run·de gayt owf mikh
Cheers!	Prost!
	prawst

Buying Food

How much is (a kilo of cheese)?	Was kostet (ein Kilo Käse)?
	vas kos·tet (ain kee·lo kay·ze)
What's that?	Was ist das?
	vas ist das
Can I taste it?	Kann ich das probieren?
	kan ikh das pro·bee·ren

PHRASE BUILDER

I'd like ...	Ich möchte ...	*ikh merkh·te ...*
(100) grams	(hundert) Gramm	*(hun·dert) gram*
(two) kilos	(zwei) Kilo	*(tsvai) kee·lo*
(three) pieces	(drei) Stück	*(drai) shtük*
(six) slices	(sechs) Scheiben	*(zeks) shai·ben*
some ...	etwas ...	*et·vas ...*

Less.	Weniger.
	vay·ni·ger
Enough.	Genug.
	ge·nook
A bit more.	Ein bisschen mehr.
	ain bis·khen mair

Menu Decoder

This miniguide to German cuisine is designed to help you navigate menus. German nouns, and adjectives affected by gender, have their gender indicated by ⓜ, ⓕ or ⓝ. If it's a plural noun, you'll also see pl.

- a -

Aal ⓜ ahl eel
Alkoholfreie Getränke ⓝ pl al·ko·*hawl*·frai·e ge·*treng*·ke soft drinks
Aperitifs ⓜ pl a·pe·ri·*teefs* aperitifs
Apfel ⓜ *ap*·fel apple
Apfelsine ⓕ ap·fel·*zee*·ne orange
Aprikose ⓕ a·pri·*kaw*·ze apricot
Artischocke ⓕ ar·ti·*sho*·ke artichoke
Auflauf ⓝ *owf*·lowf casserole • soufflé
Auster ⓕ *ows*·ter oyster

- b -

Bäckerofen ⓜ be·ker·aw·fen 'baker's oven' – baked pork & lamb dish
Backhähnchen ⓝ *bak*·hayn·khen fried chicken
Backpflaume ⓕ *bak*·pflow·me prune
Banane ⓕ ba·*nah*·ne banana
Barsch ⓜ barsh perch
Bayrisch Kraut ⓝ *bai*·rish krowt shredded cabbage cooked with apples, wine & sugar
Beefsteak ⓝ *beef*·stayk hamburger patty
Beilagen ⓕ pl *bai*·lah·gen side dishes
Berliner ⓜ ber·*lee*·ner jam doughnut

Bienenstich ⓜ bee·nen·shtikh cake with a coating of almonds & sugar
Bier ⓝ beer beer
Birne ⓕ *bir*·ne pear
Bischofsbrot ⓝ bi·shofs·brawt fruit & nut cake
Blaubeere ⓕ *blow*·bair·re bilberry • blueberry
Blaukraut ⓝ *blow*·krowt red cabbage
Blumenkohl ⓜ *bloo*·men·kawl cauliflower
Blutwurst ⓕ *bloot*·vurst blood sausage
Bockwurst ⓕ *bok*·vurst pork sausage
Bohnen ⓕ pl *baw*·nen beans
Bratwurst ⓕ *braht*·vurst fried pork sausage
Brezel ⓕ *bray*·tsel pretzel
Brokkoli ⓜ pl bro·ko·li broccoli
Brombeere ⓕ *brom*·bair·re blackberry
Brot ⓝ brawt bread
Brötchen ⓝ *brert*·khen bread roll
Bulette ⓕ bu·*le*·te meatball (Berlin)

- c -

Cervelatwurst ⓕ ser·ve·*laht*·vurst spicy pork & beef sausage
Cremespeise ⓕ *kraym*·shpai·ze mousse

- d -

Damenkäse ⓜ *dah*·men·kay·ze soft, buttery cheese
Dampfnudeln ① pl *dampf*·noo·deln hot yeast dumplings with vanilla sauce
Dattel ① *da*·tel date
Dessertweine ⓜ pl de·*sair*·vai·ne dessert wines
Digestifs ⓜ pl di·zhes·*teefs* digestifs
Dorsch ⓜ dorsh cod

- e -

Ei ⓝ ai egg
Eierkuchen ⓝ *ai*·er·koo·khen pancake
Eintopf ⓜ *ain*·topf stew
Eis ⓝ ais ice cream
Eisbein ⓝ *ais*·bain pickled pork knuckles
Ente ① *en*·te duck
Erbse ① *erp*·se pea
Erbsensuppe ① *erp*·sen·zu·pe pea soup
Erdäpfel ⓜ pl *ert*·ep·fel potatoes
Erdbeere ① *ert*·bair·re strawberry
Erdnuss ① *ert*·nus peanut
Essig ⓜ *e*·sikh vinegar

- f -

Fasan ⓜ fa·*zahn* pheasant
Feige ① *fai*·ge fig
Filet ⓝ fi·*lay* fillet
Fisch ⓜ fish fish
Fladen ⓜ *flah*·den round, flat dough cake
Flädle ⓜ pl *flayt*·le thin strips of pancake, added to soup
Fleisch ⓝ flaish meat
Forelle ① fo·*re*·le trout
Frikadelle ① fri·ka·*de*·le meatball

Frucht ① frukht fruit
Frühlingssuppe ① *frü*·lingks·zu·pe vegetable soup
Frühstücksspeck ⓜ *frü*·shtüks·shpek bacon

- g -

Gans ① gans goose
Garnele ① gar·*nay*·le prawn • shrimp
Gebäck ⓝ ge·*bek* pastries
Geflügel ⓝ ge·*flü*·gel poultry
gekocht ge·*kokht* boiled • cooked
Gemüse ⓝ ge·*mü*·ze vegetables
geräuchert ge·*roy*·khert smoked
Granat ⓜ gra·*naht* shrimp
Granatapfel ⓜ gra·*naht*·ap·fel pomegranate
Graupensuppe ① *grow*·pen·zu·pe barley soup
Grießklößchensuppe ①
grees·klers·khen·zu·pe soup with semolina dumplings
grüner Salat ⓜ *grü*·ner za·*laht* green salad
Gurke ① *gur*·ke cucumber • gherkin

- h -

Hähnchen ⓝ *hayn*·khen chicken
Hämchen ⓝ *hem*·khen pork hock or shank, served with sauerkraut & potatoes
Hase ⓜ *hah*·ze hare
Haselnuß ① *hah*·zel·nus hazelnut
Hauptgerichte ⓝ pl *howpt*·ge·rikh·te main courses
Hecht ⓜ hekht pike
Heidelbeere ① *hai*·del·bair·re bilberry • blueberry
Heilbutt ⓜ *hail*·but halibut
Hering ⓜ *hay*·ring herring
Himbeere ① *him*·bair·re raspberry
Hirsch ⓜ hirsh male deer
Honig ⓜ *haw*·nikh honey

47

Hörnchen ⓝ *hern*·khen croissant
Hühnerbrust ⓕ *hü*·ner·brust chicken breast
Hühnersuppe ⓕ *hü*·ner·zu·pe chicken soup
Hummer ⓜ *hu*·mer lobster

- j -

Joghurt ⓜ *yaw*·gurt yogurt

- k -

Kabeljau ⓜ *kah*·bel·yow cod
Kaiserschmarren ⓜ *kai*·zer·shmar·ren pancakes with raisins, served with fruit compote or chocolate sauce
Kalbfleisch ⓝ *kalp*·flaish veal
Kaninchen ⓝ ka·*neen*·khen rabbit
Karotte ⓕ ka·*ro*·te carrot
Karpfen ⓜ *karp*·fen carp
Kartoffel ⓕ kar·*to*·fel potato
Käse ⓜ *kay*·ze cheese
Kasseler ⓜ *kas*·ler smoked pork
Katenwurst ⓕ *kah*·ten·vurst country-style smoked sausage
Katzenjammer ⓜ ka·*tsen*·ya·mer cold slices of beef in mayonnaise with cucumbers or gherkin
Keule ⓕ *koy*·le haunch • leg
Kieler Sprotten ⓕ pl *kee*·ler *shpro*·ten small smoked herring
Kirsche ⓕ *kir*·she cherry
Klöße ⓜ pl *kler*·se dumplings
Knackwurst ⓕ *knak*·vurst sausage lightly flavoured with garlic
Knoblauch ⓜ *knawp*·lowkh garlic
Knödel ⓜ *kner*·del dumpling
Kohl ⓜ kawl cabbage
Kompott ⓝ kom·*pot* stewed fruit
Königinsuppe ⓕ *ker*·ni·gin·zu·pe creamy chicken soup with pieces of chicken

Königstorte ⓕ *ker*·niks·tor·te rum-flavoured fruit cake
Kopfsalat ⓜ *kopf*·za·laht lettuce
Kotelett ⓝ kot·*let* chop
Krabbe ⓕ *kra*·be crab
Krakauer ⓕ *krah*·kow·er thick, paprika-spiced sausage of Polish origin
Kraut ⓝ krowt cabbage
Kräuter ⓜ pl *kroy*·ter herbs
Krebs ⓜ krayps crab • crayfish
Krokette ⓕ kro·*ke*·te croquette
Kuchen ⓜ *koo*·khen cake
Kümmel ⓜ *kü*·mel caraway (seeds)
Kürbis ⓜ *kür*·bis pumpkin
Kutteln ⓕ pl *ku*·teln tripe

- l -

Lachs ⓜ laks salmon
Lammfleisch ⓝ *lam*·flaish lamb
Landjäger ⓜ *lant*·yay·ger thin, long, hard, spicy sausage
Languste ⓕ lan·*gus*·te crayfish
Lauch ⓜ lowkh leek
Leber ⓕ *lay*·ber liver
Leberkäse ⓜ *lay*·ber·kay·ze seasoned meatloaf made of minced liver, pork & bacon
Leberwurst ⓕ *lay*·ber·vurst liver sausage
Lebkuchen ⓜ *layp*·koo·khen gingerbread
Leckerli ⓝ *le*·ker·lee honey-flavoured ginger biscuit
Lende ⓕ *len*·de loin
Limburger ⓜ *lim*·bur·ger strong cheese flavoured with herbs
Linsen ⓕ pl *lin*·zen lentils
Linzer Torte ⓕ *lin*·tser tor·te latticed tart with jam topping
Lorbeerblätter ⓝ pl *lor*·bair·ble·ter bay leaves

Lucullus-Eier ⓝ pl lu·*ku*·lus·ai·er
poached, boiled or scrambled eggs
with goose liver, truffle & other
garnishes

- m -

Mais ⓜ mais sweet corn
Majonnaise ⓕ ma·yo·*nay*·ze
mayonnaise
Makrele ⓕ ma·*kray*·le mackerel
Mandarine ⓕ man·da·*ree*·ne
mandarine • tangerine
Mandel ⓕ *man*·del almond
Marmelade ⓕ mar·me·*lah*·de jam
Matjes ⓜ *mat*·yes young herring
Meeresfrüchte ⓕ pl
mair·res·frükh·te seafood
Meerrettich ⓜ *mair*·re·tikh
horseradish
Mehl ⓝ mayl flour
Mett ⓜ met lean minced pork
Milch ⓕ milkh milk
Möhre ⓕ *mer*·re carrot
Müesli ⓝ *mü*·es·li muesli
Muschel ⓕ *mu*·shel clam • mussel
Muskat ⓜ mus·*kaht* nutmeg
Müsli ⓝ *müs*·li muesli

- n -

Nachspeisen ⓕ pl *nahkh*·shpai·zen
desserts
Nelken ⓕ pl *nel*·ken cloves
Niere ⓕ *nee*·re kidney
Nudelauflauf ⓜ *noo*·del·owf·lowf
pasta casserole
Nudeln ⓕ pl *noo*·deln noodles

- o -

Obatzter ⓜ *aw*·bats·ter Bavarian
soft cheese mousse

Obst ⓝ awpst fruit
Ochsenschwanz ⓜ *ok*·sen·shvants
oxtail

- p -

Palatschinken ⓜ pa·*lat*·shing·ken
pancake, usually filled with jam or
cheese
Pampelmuse ⓕ pam·pel·*moo*·ze
grapefruit
Paprika ⓕ *pap*·ri·kah sweet pepper
Pastetchen ⓝ pas·*tayt*·khen filled
puff-pastry case
Pastete ⓕ pas·*tay*·te pastry • pie
Pellkartoffeln ⓕ pl *pel*·kar·to·feln
small jacket potatoes served in their
skins
Petersilie ⓕ pay·ter·*zee*·li·e parsley
Pfannkuchen ⓜ *pfan*·koo·khen
pancake
Pfeffer ⓜ *pfe*·fer pepper
Pfifferling ⓜ *pfi*·fer·ling chanterelle
mushroom
Pfirsich ⓜ *pfir*·zikh peach
Pflaume ⓕ *pflow*·me plum
Pichelsteiner ⓜ *pi*·khel·shtai·ner
meat & vegetable stew
Pilz ⓜ pilts mushroom
Pökelfleisch ⓝ *per*·kel·flaish
marinated meat
Pommes Frites pl pom frit French
fries
Porree ⓜ *por*·ray leek
Preiselbeere ⓕ *prai*·zel·bair·re
cranberry
Printe ⓕ *prin*·te honey-flavoured
biscuit
Pumpernickel ⓜ *pum*·per·ni·kel very
dark bread made with rye
Putenbrust ⓕ *poo*·ten·brust turkey
breast
Puter ⓜ *poo*·ter turkey

- q -

Quark ⓜ kvark quark (curd cheese)
Quitte ⓕ kvi·te quince

- r -

Radieschen ⓝ ra·dees·khen radish
Ragout ⓝ ra·goo stew
Rahm ⓜ rahm cream
Rebhuhn ⓝ rayp·hoon partridge
Regensburger ⓜ ray·gens·bur·ger highly spiced smoked sausage
Reh ⓝ ray venison
Reibekuchen ⓝ rai·be·koo·khen potato cake
Reis ⓜ rais rice
Rettich ⓜ re·tikh radish
Rhabarber ⓜ ra·bar·ber rhubarb
Rindfleisch ⓝ rint·flaish beef
Rippenspeer ⓜ ri·pen·shpair spare ribs
Rogen ⓜ raw·gen roe
Roggenbrot ⓝ ro·gen·brawt rye bread
Rollmops ⓜ rol·mops pickled herring fillet rolled around chopped onions or gherkins
Rosenkohl ⓜ raw·zen·kawl Brussels sprouts
Rosinen ⓕ pl ro·zee·nen raisins
Rosmarin ⓜ raws·ma·reen rosemary
Rotweine ⓜ pl rawt·vai·ne red wines
Roulade ⓕ ru·lah·de slices of beef stuffed with onion, bacon and dill pickles, then rolled & braised
Rühreier ⓝ pl rür·ai·er scrambled eggs
Russische Eier ⓝ pl ru·si·she ai·er 'Russian eggs' – eggs with mayonnaise

- s -

Sahne ⓕ zah·ne cream
Salat ⓜ za·laht salad
Salz ⓝ zalts salt
Salzkartoffeln ⓕ pl zalts·kar·to·feln boiled potatoes
Sauerbraten ⓜ zow·er·brah·ten marinated roasted beef served with a sour cream sauce
Sauerkraut ⓝ zow·er·krowt pickled cabbage
Schaumweine ⓜ pl showm·vai·ne sparkling wines
Schellfisch ⓜ shel·fish haddock
Schinken ⓜ shing·ken ham
Schlachtplatte ⓕ shlakht·pla·te selection of pork & sausage
Schmorbraten ⓜ shmawr·brah·ten beef pot roast
Schnittlauch ⓜ shnit·lowkh chives
Schnitzel ⓝ shni·tsel pork, veal or chicken breast pounded flat, covered in breadcrumbs & pan-fried
Scholle ⓕ sho·le plaice
Schwarzwälder Kirschtorte ⓕ shvarts·vel·der kirsh·tor·te Black Forest cake
Schwein ⓝ shvain pork
Seezunge ⓕ zay·tsung·e sole
Sekt ⓜ zekt sparkling wine
Selchfleisch ⓝ zelkh·flaish smoked pork
Sellerie ⓕ ze·le·ree celery
Senf ⓜ zenf mustard
Soße ⓕ zaw·se gravy • sauce
Spanferkel ⓝ shpahn·fer·kel suckling pig
Spargel ⓜ shpar·gel asparagus
Spätzle pl shpets·le thick noodles
Speck ⓜ shpek bacon
Spekulatius ⓜ shpe·ku·lah·tsi·us almond biscuits

Spiegelei ⓝ *shpee*-gel-ai fried egg
Spinat ⓜ shpi-*naht* spinach
Spirituosen pl shpi-ri-tu-*aw*-zen
spirits
Sprossenkohl ⓜ *shpro*-sen-kawl
Brussels sprout
Sprotten ⓕ pl *shpro*-ten sprats
(small herring-like fish)
Steckrübe ⓕ *shtek*-rü-be turnip
Steinbutt ⓜ *shtain*-but turbot
(flatfish)
Stelze ⓕ *shtel*-tse knuckle of pork
Streuselkuchen ⓜ
shtroy-zel-koo-khen coffee cake
topped with a mixture of butter,
sugar, flour & cinnamon
Strudel ⓜ *shtroo*-del loaf-shaped
pastry filled with a sweet or savoury
filling
Suppe ⓕ *zu*-pe soup

- t -

Teigwaren pl *taik*-vah-ren pasta
Thunfisch ⓜ *toon*-fish tuna
Thüringer ⓕ *tü*-ring-er long, thin,
spiced sausage
Thymian ⓜ *tü*-mi-ahn thyme
Toast ⓜ *tawst* toast
Tomate ⓕ to-*mah*-te tomato
Törtchen ⓝ *tert*-khen small tart
or cake
Torte ⓕ *tor*-te layer cake
Truthahn ⓜ *troot*-hahn turkey
Tunke ⓕ *tung*-ke gravy • sauce

- v -

Voressen ⓝ *fawr*-e-sen meat stew
Vorspeisen ⓕ pl *fawr*-shpai-zen
appetizers

- w -

Wachtel ⓕ *vakh*-tel quail
Walnuss ⓕ *val*-nus walnut
Weichkäse ⓜ *vaikh*-kay-ze soft
cheese
Weinkraut ⓝ *vain*-krowt white
cabbage, braised with apples &
simmered in wine
Weintraube ⓕ *vain*-trow-be grape
Weißbrot ⓝ *vais*-brawt white bread
Weißweine ⓜ pl *vais*-vai-ne white
wines
Weißwurst ⓕ *vais*-vurst veal sausage
Wiener Schnitzel ⓝ vee-ner *shni*-tsel
crumbed veal
Wild ⓝ *vilt* game (meat)
Wurst ⓕ *vurst* sausage
Wurstplatte ⓕ *vurst*-pla-te cold cuts

- z -

Ziege ⓕ *tsee*-ge goat
Zitrone ⓕ tsi-*traw*-ne lemon
Zucker ⓜ *tsu*-ker sugar
Zunge ⓕ *tsung*-e tongue
Zwetschge ⓕ *tsvetsh*-ge plum
Zwiebel ⓕ *tsvee*-bel onion
Zwischenrippenstück ⓝ
tsvi-shen-ri-pen-shtük rib eye steak

Sightseeing

≋ Fast Phrases

When's the museum open?	Wann hat das Museum geöffnet? *van hat das mu·zay·um ge·erf·net*
When's the next tour?	Wann ist die nächste Tour? *van ist dee naykhs·te toor*
Can I take photos?	Kann ich fotografieren? *kan ikh fo·to·gra·fee·ren*

Planning

Do you have information on local sights?	Haben Sie Informationen über örtliche Sehenswürdigkeiten? *hah·ben zee in·for·ma·tsyaw·nen ü·ber ert·li·khe zay·ens·vür·dikh·kai·ten*
I only have (one day).	Ich habe nur (einen Tag). *ikh hah·be noor (ai·nen tahk)*
I'd like to see ...	Ich möchte ... sehen. *ikh merkh·te ... zay·en*
I'd like an audio set.	Ich hätte gern einen Audioführer. *ikh he·te gern ai·nen ow·di·o·fü·rer*

| I'd like to hire a local guide. | Ich würde gern einen Fremdenführer anheuern.
ikh *vür*·de gern *ai*·nen *frem*·den·fü·rer *an*·ho·yern |
| **Are there guides?** | Gibt es Fremdenführer?
gipt es *frem*·den·fü·rer |

Questions

What's that?	Was ist das? vas ist das
How old is it?	Wie alt ist es? vee alt ist es
Who made it?	Wer hat das gemacht? vair hat das ge·*makht*
Can I take photos (of you)?	Kann ich (Sie/du) fotografieren? **pol/inf** kan ikh (zee/doo) fo·to·gra·*fee*·ren
Could you take a photo of me?	Könnten Sie ein Foto von mir machen? *kern*·ten zee ain *fo*·to fon meer *ma*·khen

---

PHRASE BUILDER

I'd like a/an ...	Ich hätte gern ...	ikh *he*·te gern ...
audio set	einen Audioführer	*ai*·nen ow·di·o·fü·rer
catalogue	einen Katalog	*ai*·nen ka·ta·*lawg*
guidebook (in English)	einen Reiseführer (auf Englisch)	*ai*·nen *rai*·ze·fü·rer (owf *eng*·lish)
local map	eine Karte von hier	*ai*·ne *kar*·te fon heer

Getting In

What time does it open?	Wann macht es auf?	
	van makht es owf	
What time does it close?	Wann macht es zu?	
	van makht es tsoo	
What's the admission charge?	Was kostet der Eintritt?	
	vas *kos*·tet dair *ain*·trit	

PHRASE BUILDER

Is there a discount for ...?	Gibt es eine Ermäßigung für ...?	gipt es *ai*·ne er·*may*·si·gung für ...
children	Kinder	*kin*·der
families	Familien	fa·*mee*·li·en
groups	Gruppen	*gru*·pen
older people	Senioren	*zay*·nyaw·ren
students	Studenten	shtu·*den*·ten

Galleries & Museums

When's the gallery open?	Wann hat die Galerie geöffnet?
	van hat dee ga·le·*ree* ge·*erf*·net
When's the museum open?	Wann hat das Museum geöffnet?
	van hat das mu·*zay*·um ge·*erf*·net
What's in the collection?	Was gibt es in der Sammlung?
	vas gipt es in dair *zam*·lung
It's a/an ... exhibition.	Es ist eine ...-Ausstellung.
	es ist *ai*·ne ...·*ows*·shte·lung

54

| I like the works of ... | Ich mag die Arbeiten von ... |
| | ikh mahk dee *ar*·bai·ten fon ... |

... **art**	... Kunst	... kunst
baroque	barocke	ba·*ro*·ke
expressionist	expressionist-ische	eks·pre·syo·*nist*·i·she
Gothic	gotische	*gaw*·ti·she
modernist	moderne	mo·*der*·ne

Tours

When's the next excursion?	Wann ist der nächste Ausflug?
	van ist dair *naykhs*·te *ows*·flook
When's the next tour?	Wann ist der nächste Tour?
	van ist dair *naykhs*·te toor
Is food included?	Ist das Essen inbegriffen?
	ist das *e*·sen *in*·be·gri·fen
Is transport included?	Ist die Beförderung inbegriffen?
	ist dee be·*fer*·de·rung *in*·be·gri·fen

Fast Talk **Forming Sentences**

You don't need to memorise complete sentences; instead, simply use key words to get your meaning across. For example, you might know that *wann* van means 'when' in German. So if you've arranged a tour but don't know at what time, just ask *Tour wann?* toor van. Don't worry that you're not getting the whole sentence right – people will understand if you stick to the key words.

Can you recommend a tour?	Können Sie eine Tour empfehlen? *ker*·nen zee *ai*·ne toor emp·*fay*·len
Can you recommend a boat trip?	Können Sie eine Bootsrundfahrt empfehlen? *ker*·nen zee *ai*·ne *bawts*·runt·fahrt emp·*fay*·len
Can you recommend a day trip?	Können Sie ein Tagesausflug empfehlen? *ker*·nen zee ain *tah*·ges·ows·flook emp·*fay*·len

Do I need to take ... with me?	Muss ich ... mitnehmen? mus ikh ... *mit*·nay·men
How long is the tour?	Wie lange dauert die Führung? vee *lang*·e *dow*·ert dee *fü*·rung
What time should we be back?	Wann sollen wir zurück sein? van *zo*·len veer tsu·*rük* zain
I've lost my group.	Ich habe meine Gruppe verloren. ikh *hah*·be *mai*·ne *gru*·pe fer·*law*·ren

Shopping

Fast Phrases

Can I look at it?	Können Sie es mir zeigen? *ker*·nen zee es meer *tsai*·gen
How much is this?	Wie viel kostet das? vee feel *kos*·tet das
That's too expensive.	Das ist zu teuer. das ist tsoo *toy*·er

Looking For ...

Where's (a market)?	Wo ist (ein Markt)? vaw ist (ain markt)
Where can I buy (locally produced goods)?	Wo kann ich (örtlich produzierte Waren) kaufen? vaw kan ikh (*ert*·likh pro·du·*tseer*·te *vah*·ren) *kow*·fen

In the Shop

I'd like to buy ...	Ich möchte ... kaufen. ikh *merkh*·te ... *kow*·fen
I'm just looking.	Ich schaue mich nur um. ikh *show*·e mikh noor um

Where would you go for bargains?	Wo kann man Schnäppchen machen? vaw kan man *shnep*·khen *ma*·khen
Where would you go for souvenirs?	Wo kann man Souvenirs kaufen? vaw kan man zu·ve·*neers* *kow*·fen

Can I look at it?	Können Sie es mir zeigen? *ker*·nen zee es meer *tsai*·gen
What is this made from?	Woraus ist das gemacht? vaw·*rows* ist das ge·*makht*
Do you have any others?	Haben Sie noch andere? *hah*·ben zee nokh *an*·de·re
It's faulty.	Es ist fehlerhaft. es ist *fay*·ler·haft
It's broken.	Es ist kaputt. es ist ka·*put*
Can I have it wrapped?	Könnte ich es eingepackt bekommen? *kern*·te ikh es *ain*·ge·pakt be·*ko*·men
Can I have a bag, please?	Könnte ich eine Tüte bekommen? *kern*·te ikh *ai*·ne *tü*·te be·*ko*·men
I'd like my money back, please.	Ich möchte bitte mein Geld zurückhaben. ikh *merkh*·te *bi*·te main gelt tsu·*rük*·hah·ben

| I'd like to return this, please. | Ich möchte bitte dieses zurückgeben.
ikh *merkh*·te *bi*·te *dee*·zes tsu·*rük*·gay·ben |

Paying & Bargaining

How much is this?	Wie viel kostet das? vee feel *kos*·tet das
How much?	Das kostet? das *kos*·tet
It's (30) euros.	Das kostet (dreißig) Euro. das *kos*·tet (*drai*·tsikh) *oy*·ro
Can you write down the price?	Können Sie den Preis aufschreiben? *ker*·nen zee dayn prais *owf*·shrai·ben
That's too expensive.	Das ist zu teuer. das ist tsoo *toy*·er
Do you have something cheaper?	Haben Sie etwas Billigeres? *hah*·ben zee *et*·vas *bi*·li·ge·res
I'll give you ...	Ich gebe Ihnen ... ikh *gay*·be *ee*·nen ...
Do you accept credit cards cards?	Nehmen Sie Kreditkarten? *nay*·men zee kre·*deet*·kar·ten
Can I have a receipt, please?	Könnte ich eine Quittung bekommen? *kern*·te ikh *ai*·ne *kvi*·tung be·*ko*·men
Receipt, please.	Eine Quittung, bitte. *ai*·ne *kvi*·tung *bi*·te

| I'd like my change, please. | Ich möchte bitte mein Wechselgeld. |
| | ikh *merkh*·te *bi*·te main *vek*·sel·gelt |

Clothes & Shoes

I'm looking for shoes/ underwear.	Ich suche nach Schuhen/ Unterwäsche.
	ikh *zoo*·khe nahkh *shoo*·en/ *un*·ter·ve·she
My size is (40).	Ich habe Größe (vierzig).
	ikh *hah*·be *grer*·se (*feer*·tsikh)
small	klein
	klain
medium	mittelgroß
	mi·tel·graws
large	groß
	graws
Can I try it on?	Kann ich es anprobieren?
	kan ikh es *an*·pro·bee·ren
It doesn't fit.	Es passt nicht.
	es past nikht

Fast Talk **False Friends**

Some German words look like English words but have a different meaning altogether. For example, *Chef* shef is 'boss' (not 'chef', which is *Koch* kokh); *Tip* tip is 'advance information' (not 'bonus payment', which is *Trinkgeld* trink·gelt); *komisch kaw*·mish is 'strange' (not 'comical', which is *lustig lus*·tikh); and *blank* blank is 'shiny' (not 'blank', which is *leer* leer).

Books & Reading

Is there an English-language bookshop?	Gibt es einen Buchladen für englische Bücher? gipt es *ai*·nen bookh·*lah*·den für *eng*·li·she *bü*·kher
Is there an English-language section?	Gibt es eine Abteilung für englische Bücher? gipt es *ai*·ne ap·*tai*·lung für *eng*·li·she *bü*·kher
I'm looking for something by ...	Ich suche nach etwas von ... ikh *zoo*·khe nahkh *et*·vas fon ...
I'd like a dictionary.	Ich hätte gerne ein Wörterbuch. ikh *he*·te *ger*·ne ain *ver*·ter·bookh
I'd like a newspaper (in English).	Ich hätte gerne eine Zeitung (in Englisch). ikh *he*·te *ger*·ne *ai*·ne *tsai*·tung (in *eng*·lish)

Music & DVDs

I'd like a CD/DVD.	Ich hätte gern eine CD/DVD. ikh *he*·te gern *ai*·ne tsay·*day*/day·fow·*day*
I'd like some headphones.	Ich hätte gern Kopfhörer. ikh *he*·te gern *kopf*·her·rer
What's their best recording?	Was ist ihre beste CD? vas ist *ee*·re *bes*·te tsay·*day*
Can I listen to this?	Kann ich mir das anhören? kan ikh meer das *an*·her·ren
What region is this DVD for?	Für welche Region ist diese DVD? für *vel*·khe re·*gyawn* ist *dee*·ze day·fow·*day*

Entertainment

≡ Fast Phrases

What's on tonight?	Was ist heute Abend los? vas ist *hoy*·te *ah*·bent laws
Where are the clubs?	Wo sind die Klubs? vaw zint dee klups
When/Where shall we meet?	Wann/Wo sollen wir uns treffen? van/vaw *zo*·len veer uns *tre*·fen

Going Out

What's there to do in the evenings?	Was kann man abends unternehmen? vas kan man *ah*·bents un·ter·*nay*·men
What's on today?	Was ist heute los? vas ist *hoy*·te laws
What's on tonight?	Was ist heute Abend los? vas ist *hoy*·te *ah*·bent laws
What's on this weekend?	Was ist dieses Wochenende los? vas ist *dee*·zes *vo*·khen·en·de laws
✂ **What's on?**	Was ist los? vas ist laws

62

Fast Talk **Addressing People**

There's no equivalent of the English 'Ms' in German – all women should be addressed using *Frau* frow, just like *Herr* her (Mr) applies to all men. The term *Fräulein* froy·lain (Miss) is only used today to address girls (and sometimes female waiters). The equivalents of 'Sir' and 'Madam', *Mein Herr* main her and *Meine Dame* mai·ne dah·me, are old-fashioned.

Is there a local entertainment guide?	Gibt es einen Veranstaltungs-kalender?
	gipt es ai·nen fer·an·shtal·tungs·ka·len·der
Is there a local gay guide?	Gibt es einen Führer für die Schwulen- und Lesbenszene?
	gipt es ai·nen fü·rer für dee shvoo·len unt les·bens·tsay·ne

PHRASE BUILDER

I feel like going to a/the ...	Ich hätte Lust, ... zu gehen.	ikh he·te lust ... tsoo gay·en
ballet	zum Ballett	tsum ba·let
bar/pub	in eine Kneipe	in ai·ne knai·pe
cafe	in ein Café	in ain ka·fay
concert	in ein Konzert	in ain kon·tsert
movies	ins Kino	ins kee·no
nightclub	in einen Nachtklub	in ai·nen nakht·klup
opera	in die Oper	in dee aw·per
restaurant	in ein Restaurant	in ain res·to·rang
theatre	ins Theater	ins te·ah·ter

Clubs

Can you recommend clubs?	Können Sie Klubs empfehlen? *ker*·nen zee klups emp-*fay*·len
Can you recommend gay venues?	Können Sie Schwulen- und Lesbenkneipen empfehlen? *ker*·nen zee *shvoo*·len unt *les*·ben·knai·pen emp-*fay*·len
Can you recommend pubs?	Können Sie Kneipen empfehlen? *ker*·nen zee *knai*·pen emp-*fay*·len

Meeting Up

When shall we meet?	Wann sollen wir uns treffen? van *zo*·len veer uns *tre*·fen
Let's meet at (eight) o'clock.	Wir treffen uns um (acht) Uhr. veer *tre*·fen uns um (akht) oor
Where shall we meet?	Wo sollen wir uns treffen? vaw *zo*·len veer uns *tre*·fen
Let's meet at the entrance.	Wir treffen uns am Eingang. veer *tre*·fen uns am *ain*·gang
Where will you be?	Wo wirst du sein? vaw virst doo zain
Sorry I'm late.	Es tut mir Leid, dass ich zu spät komme. es toot meer lait das ikh tsoo shpayt *ko*·me

Practicalities

≡ Fast Phrases

Where's the nearest ATM?	Wo ist der nächste Geldautomat? vaw ist dair *naykhs*·te *gelt*·ow·to·maht
Is there wireless internet access here?	Gibt es hier einen WLAN-Zugang? geept es heer *ai*·nen *vay*·lahn·tsoo·gang
Where's the toilet?	Wo ist die Toilette? vo ist dee to·a·*le*·te

Banking

Where's a bank?	Wo ist eine Bank? vaw ist *ai*·ne bangk
What time does the bank open?	Wann macht die Bank auf? van makht dee bangk owf
Where's the nearest ATM?	Wo ist der nächste Geldautomat? vaw ist dair *naykhs*·te *gelt*·ow·to·maht
Where's the nearest foreign exchange office?	Wo ist die nächste Geldwechselstube? vaw ist dee *naykhs*·te *gelt*·vek·sel·shtoo·be

Where can I (change money)?	Wo kann ich (Geld umtauschen)? *vaw kan ikh* (gelt *um·tow·shen*)
I'd like to (withdraw money).	Ich möchte (Geld abheben). *ikh merkh·te* (gelt *ap·hay·ben*)
What's the exchange rate?	Wie ist der Wechselkurs? *vee ist dair vek·sel·kurs*
What's the charge for that?	Wie hoch sind die Gebühren dafür? *vee hawkh zint dee ge·bü·ren da·für*

Phone/Mobile Phone

Where's the nearest public phone?	Wo ist das nächste öffentliche Telefon? *vaw ist das naykhs·te er·fent·li·khe te·le·fawn*
I want to buy a phonecard.	Ich möchte eine Telefonkarte kaufen. *ikh merkh·te ai·ne te·le·fawn·kar·te kow·fen*

Fast Talk **Reading German**

The great thing about German spelling is that the relationship between the letters and the sounds they represent is consistent, so once you become familiar with them, you should be able to pronounce a new word without a hitch. Just remember that the letter ß stands for *ss* (but the rules for when you can use ß or *ss* are confusing to Germans themselves, so you can ignore these!). Vowels written with two dots above them are pronounced differently from ordinary vowels: *ä* is like the air in 'hair', *ö* is like the er in 'teacher', and *ü* is like the ee in 'see' but pronounced with rounded lips.

I want to make a call to (Singapore).	Ich möchte nach (Singapur) telefonieren.
	ikh *merkh*·te nahkh (*zing*·a·poor) te·le·fo·*nee*·ren
I want to make a reverse charges/collect call.	Ich möchte ein R-Gespräch führen.
	ikh *merkh*·te ain *air*·ge·shpraykh *fü*·ren
How much is a (three)-minute call?	Wie viel kostet ein (drei)-minutiges Gespräch?
	vee feel *kos*·tet ain (drai)·*mi*·noo·ti·ges ge·*shpraykh*
The number is ...	Die Nummer ist ...
	dee *nu*·mer ist ...
I've been cut off.	Ich bin unterbrochen worden.
	ikh bin un·ter·*bro*·khen *vor*·den
I'd like a charger for my phone.	Ich hätte gern ein Ladegerät für mein Handy.
	ikh *he*·te gern ain *lah*·de·ge·rayt für main *hen*·di
I'd like a SIM card for your network.	Ich hätte gern eine SIM-Karte für Ihr Netz.
	ikh *he*·te gern *ai*·ne *zim*·kar·te für eer nets

Internet

Where's the local internet cafe?	Wo ist hier ein Internet-Café?
	vaw ist heer ain *in*·ter·net·ka·fay
Is there wireless internet access here?	Gibt es hier einen WLAN-Zugang?
	geept es heer *ai*·nen *vay*·lahn·tsoo·gang

Can I connect my laptop here?	Kann ich meinen Laptop hier anschließen? kan ikh *mai*·nen *lep*·top heer *an*·shlee·sen
Do you have headphones (with a microphone)?	Haben Sie Kopfhörer (mit einem Mikrofon)? *hah*·ben zee *kopf*·her·rer (mit *ai*·nem *mee*·kro·fawn)

PHRASE BUILDER

I'd like to ...	Ich möchte ...	ikh *merkh*·te ...
burn a CD	eine CD brennen	*ai*·ne tsay·*day* *bre*·nen
check my email	meine E-Mails checken	*mai*·ne *ee*·mayls *che*·ken
download my photos	meine Fotos herunterladen	*mai*·ne *faw*·tos he·*run*·ter·lah·den
use a printer	einen Drucker benutzen	*ai*·nen *dru*·ker be·*nu*·tsen
use a scanner	einen Scanner benutzen	*ai*·nen *ske*·ner be·*nu*·tsen
use Skype	Skype benutzen	skaip be·*nu*·tsen

How much per hour/page?	Was kostet es pro Stunde/Seite? vas *kos*·tet es praw *shtun*·de/*zai*·te
How do I log on?	Wie logge ich mich ein? vee *law*·ge ikh mikh ain
It's crashed.	Es ist abgestürzt. es ist *ap*·ge·shtürtst
I've finished.	Ich bin fertig. ikh bin *fer*·tikh

Can I connect (my camera) to this computer?	Kann ich (meine Kamera) an diesen Computer anschließen? kan ikh (mai·ne kah·me·ra) an dee·zen kom·pyoo·ter an·shlee·sen

Emergencies

Help!	Hilfe! hil·fe
Stop!	Halt! halt
Go away!	Gehen Sie weg! gay·en zee vek
Leave me alone!	Lass mich zufrieden! las mikh tsu·free·den
Thief!	Dieb! deeb
Fire!	Feuer! foy·er
Watch out!	Vorsicht! for·zikht
It's an emergency!	Es ist ein Notfall! es ist ain nawt·fal
Call the police!	Rufen Sie die Polizei! roo·fen zee dee po·li·tsai
Call a doctor!	Rufen Sie einen Arzt! roo·fen zee ai·nen artst
There's been an accident.	Es gab einen Unfall. es gahp ai·nen un·fal

PRACTICALITIES

Fast Talk **Understanding German**

Most sentences are composed of several words (or parts of words) serving various grammatical functions, as well as those that carry meaning (primarily nouns and verbs). If you're finding it hard to understand what someone is saying to you, listen out for the nouns and verbs to work out the context – this shouldn't be hard as they are usually more emphasised in speech. If you're still having trouble, a useful phrase to know is *Könnten Sie bitte langsamer sprechen? kern*·ten zee *bi*·te *lang*·za·mer *shpre*·khen (Please speak more slowly).

Do you have a first-aid kit?	Haben Sie einen Erste-Hilfe-Kasten? *hah*·ben zee *ai*·nen ayr·ste·*hil*·fe·ka·sten
Could you please help me/us?	Könnten Sie mir/uns bitte helfen? *kern*·ten zee meer/uns *bi*·te *hel*·fen
Please help!	Bitte helfen! *bi*·te *hel*·fen
I have to use the telephone.	Ich muss das Telefon benutzen. ikh mus das te·le·*fawn* be·*nu*·tsen
Where are the toilets?	Wo ist die Toilette? vo ist dee to·a·*le*·te
I'm lost.	Ich habe mich verirrt. ikh *hah*·be mikh fer·*irt*

Police

Where's the police station?	Wo ist das Polizeirevier? *vaw ist das po·li·tsai·re·veer*
I've been raped.	Ich bin vergewaltigt worden. *ikh bin fer·ge·val·tikht vor·den*
I've been robbed.	Ich bin bestohlen worden. *ikh bin be·shtaw·len vor·den*
I've lost (my bag).	Ich habe (meine Tasche) verloren. *ikh hah·be (mai·ne ta·she) fer·law·ren*
I've lost (my passport).	Ich habe (meinen Pass) verloren. *ikh hah·be (mai·nen pas) fer·law·ren*
(My money) was stolen.	Man hat mir (mein Geld) gestohlen. *man hat meer (main gelt) ge·shtaw·len*
I want to contact my consulate.	Ich möchte mich mit meinem Konsulat in Verbindung setzen. *ikh merkh·te mikh mit mai·nem kon·zu·laht in fer·bin·dung ze·tsen*
I want to contact my embassy.	Ich möchte mich mit meiner Botschaft in Verbindung setzen. *ikh merkh·te mikh mit mai·ner bawt·shaft in fer·bin·dung ze·tsen*
I have insurance.	Ich bin versichert. *ikh bin fer·zi·khert*

Health

Where's the nearest chemist?	Wo ist die nächste Apotheke?
	vaw ist dee *naykhs*·te a·po·*tay*·ke
Where's the nearest dentist?	Wo ist der nächste Zahnarzt?
	vaw ist dair *naykhs*·te *tsahn*·artst
Where's the nearest hospital?	Wo ist das nächste Krankenhaus?
	vaw ist das *naykhs*·te *krang*·ken·hows
I need a doctor (who speaks English).	Ich brauche einen Arzt (der Englisch spricht).
	ikh *brow*·khe *ai*·nen artst (dair *eng*·lish shprikht)
Could I see a female doctor?	Könnte ich von einer Ärztin behandelt werden?
	kern·te ikh fon *ai*·ner *erts*·tin be·*han*·delt *ver*·den
I'm sick.	Ich bin krank.
	ikh bin krangk
It hurts here.	Es tut hier weh.
	es toot heer *vay*

Fast Talk **Negatives**

To make a negative statement in German, just add the word *nicht* nikht (not) after the verb (or after the object if included): *ich rauche nicht* ikh *row*·khe nikht (lit: I smoke not). With nouns, the negative article *kein* kain is used instead of *nicht*: *ich sehe kein Taxi* ikh *zay*·e kain *tak*·si (lit: I see no taxi).

I've been vomiting.	Ich habe mich übergeben.
	ikh *hah*·be mikh *ü*·ber·*gay*·ben
I feel nauseous.	Mir ist übel.
	meer ist *ü*·bel
I feel dizzy.	Mir ist schwindelig.
	meer ist *shvin*·de·likh
I have a cold.	Ich bin erkältet.
	ikh bin er·*kel*·tet
I have a rash.	Ich habe einen Ausschlag.
	ikh *hah*·be *ai*·nen *ows*·shlahk
I have an infection.	Ich habe eine Infektion.
	ikh *hah*·be *ai*·ne in·fek·*tsyawn*

PHRASE BUILDER

I have a ...	Ich habe ...	ikh *hah*·be ...
cough	Husten	*hoos*·ten
fever	Fieber	*fee*·ber
headache	Kopfschmerzen	*kopf*·shmer·tsen
toothache	Zahnschmerzen	*tsahn*·shmer·tsen

I'm on medication for ...	Ich nehme Medikamente gegen ...
	ikh *nay*·me me·di·ka·*men*·te *gay*·gen ...
I need something for ...	Ich brauche etwas gegen ...
	ikh *brow*·khe *et*·vas *gay*·gen ...
My prescription is ...	Mein Rezept ist ...
	main re·*tsept* ist ...
I'm allergic to (antibiotics).	Ich bin allergisch gegen (Antibiotika).
	ikh bin a·*lair*·gish *gay*·gen (an·ti·bi·*aw*·ti·ka)

Dictionary

ENGLISH *to* GERMAN

englisch – deutsch

Nouns in this dictionary, and adjectives affected by gender, have their gender indicated by ⓕ, ⓜ or ⓝ. If it's a plural noun, you'll also see pl. Where a word that could be either a noun or a verb has no gender indicated, it's a verb.

- a -

accident Unfall ⓜ *un·*fal
accommodation Unterkunft ⓕ
*un·*ter·kunft
afternoon Nachmittag ⓜ
*nahkh·*mi·tahk
air-conditioned mit Klimaanlage ⓕ
mit *klee·*ma·an·lah·ge
airplane Flugzeug ⓝ *flook·*tsoyk
airport Flughafen ⓜ *flook·*hah·fen
airport tax Flughafengebühr ⓕ
*flook·*hah·fen·ge·bür
alarm clock Wecker ⓜ *ve·*ker
alcohol Alkohol ⓜ *al·*ko·hawl
antique Antiquität ⓕ an·ti·kvi·*tayt*

appointment Termin ⓜ ter·*meen*
arrivals Ankunft ⓕ *an·*kunft
art gallery Kunstgalerie ⓕ
*kunst·*ga·le·ree
ashtray Aschenbecher ⓜ
*a·*shen·be·kher
ATM Geldautomat ⓜ *gelt·*ow·to·maht

- b -

baby Baby ⓝ *bay·*bi
back (body) Rücken ⓜ *rü·*ken
backpack Rucksack ⓜ *ruk·*zak
bad schlecht shlekht
bag Tasche ⓕ *ta·*she
baggage Gepäck ⓝ ge·*pek*

baggage allowance Freigepäck ⓝ
frai·ge·pek

baggage claim Gepäckausgabe ⓕ
ge·pek·ows·gah·be

bakery Bäckerei ⓕ *be·ke·rai*

Band-Aid Pflaster ⓝ *pflas·ter*

bank Bank ⓕ *bangk*

bank account Bankkonto ⓝ
bangk·kon·to

bath Bad ⓝ *baht*

bathroom Badezimmer ⓝ
bah·de·tsi·mer

battery Batterie ⓕ *ba·te·ree*

beach Strand ⓜ *shtrant*

beautiful schön *shern*

beauty salon Schönheitssalon ⓜ
shern·haits·za·long

bed Bett ⓝ *bet*

bedroom Schlafzimmer ⓝ
shlahf·tsi·mer

beer Bier ⓝ *beer*

bicycle Fahrrad ⓝ *fahr·raht*

big groß *graws*

bill (account) Rechnung ⓕ
rekh·nung

birthday Geburtstag ⓜ
ge·burts·tahk

blanket Decke ⓕ *de·ke*

blood group Blutgruppe ⓕ
bloot·gru·pe

boarding house Pension ⓕ
pahng·zyawn

boarding pass Bordkarte ⓕ
bort·kar·te

boat Boot ⓝ *bawt*

book Buch ⓝ *bookh*

book (reserve) buchen *boo·khen*

booked out ausgebucht
ows·ge·bookht

bookshop Buchhandlung ⓕ
bookh·hand·lung

border Grenze ⓕ *gren·tse*

bottle Flasche ⓕ *fla·she*

box Karton ⓜ *kar·tong*

boy Junge ⓜ *yung·e*

boyfriend Freund ⓜ *froynt*

bra BH ⓜ *bay·hah*

bread Brot ⓝ *brawt*

briefcase Aktentasche ⓕ
ak·ten·ta·she

broken kaputt *ka·put*

brother Bruder ⓜ *broo·der*

building Gebäude ⓝ *ge·boy·de*

bus (city) Bus ⓜ *bus*

bus (intercity) Fernbus ⓜ *fern·bus*

bus station Busbahnhof ⓜ
bus·bahn·hawf

bus stop Bushaltestelle ⓕ
bus·hal·te·shte·le

business Geschäft ⓝ *ge·sheft*

business class Business Class ⓕ
bi·zi·nes klahs

~ C ~

cafe Café ⓝ *ka·fay*

camera Kamera ⓕ *ka·me·ra*

can (tin) Dose ⓕ *daw·ze*

cancel stornieren *shtor·nee·ren*

car Auto ⓝ *ow·to*

car hire Autoverleih ⓜ *ow·to·fer·lai*

car owner's title Fahrzeugpapiere ⓝ pl
fahr·tsoyk·pa·pee·re

car registration PKW-Zulassung ⓕ
pay·kah·vay·tsoo·la·sung

cash Bargeld ⓝ *bahr·gelt*

cashier Kassierer(in) ⓜ/ⓕ
ka·see·rer/ka·see·re·rin

chairlift (skiing) Sessellift ⓜ
ze·se·lift

change (coins) Wechselgeld ⓝ
vek·sel·gelt

change (money) wechseln *vek·seln*

change (trains) umsteigen
um·shtai·gen

check (banking) Scheck ⓜ *shek*

check (bill) Rechnung ① *rekh*·nung

check-in (desk) Abfertigungsschalter ⓜ *ap*·fer·ti·gungks·shal·ter

cheque (banking) Scheck ⓜ shek

child Kind ⓝ kint

church Kirche ① *kir*·khe

cigarette lighter Feuerzeug ⓝ *foy*·er·tsoyk

city Stadt ① shtat

city centre Innenstadt ① *i*·nen·shtat

clean sauber *zow*·ber

cleaning Reinigung ① *rai*·ni·gung

cloakroom Garderobe ① gar·*draw*·be

closed geschlossen ge·*shlo*·sen

clothing Kleidung ① *klai*·dung

coat Mantel ⓜ *man*·tel

coffee Kaffee ⓜ *ka*·fay

coins Münzen ① pl *mün*·tsen

cold kalt kalt

comfortable bequem be·*kvaym*

company Firma ① *fir*·ma

computer Computer ⓜ kom·*pyoo*·ter

condom Kondom ⓝ kon·*dawm*

confirm (a booking) bestätigen be·*shtay*·ti·gen

cook kochen *ko*·khen

cough husten *hoos*·ten

countryside Land ⓝ lant

cover charge Eintrittsgeld ⓝ *ain*·trits·gelt

crafts Handwerk ⓝ *hant*·verk

credit card Kreditkarte ① kre·*deet*·kar·te

currency exchange Geldwechsel ⓜ *gelt*·vek·sel

customs (border crossing) Zoll ⓜ tsol

- d -

date (time) Datum ⓝ *dah*·tum

date of birth Geburtsdatum ⓝ ge·*burts*·dah·tum

daughter Tochter ① *tokh*·ter

day Tag ⓜ tahk

day after tomorrow übermorgen ü·ber·*mor*·gen

day before yesterday vorgestern *fawr*·ges·tern

delay Verspätung ① fer·*shpay*·tung

delicatessen Feinkostgeschäft ⓝ *fain*·kost·ge·sheft

depart (leave) abfahren *ap*·fah·ren

department store Warenhaus ⓝ *vah*·ren·hows

departure Abfahrt ① *ap*·fahrt

deposit Anzahlung ① *an*·tsah·lung

diaper Windel ① *vin*·del

dictionary Wörterbuch ⓝ *ver*·ter·bookh

dining car Speisewagen ⓜ *shpai*·ze·vah·gen

dinner Abendessen ⓝ *ah*·bent·e·sen

direct direkt di·*rekt*

dirty schmutzig *shmu*·tsikh

discount Rabatt ⓜ ra·*bat*

doctor Arzt/Ärztin ⓜ/① artst/*erts*·tin

dog Hund ⓜ hunt

double bed Doppelbett ⓝ *do*·pel·bet

dress Kleid ⓝ klait

drink (beverage) Getränk ⓝ ge·*trengk*

drink trinken *tring*·ken

drivers licence Führerschein ⓜ *fü*·rer·shain

dry (clothes) trocknen *trok*·nen

- e -

each jede *yay*·de

early früh frü

east Osten ⓜ *os*·ten

economy class Touristenklasse ① tu·*ris*·ten·kla·se

elevator Lift ⓜ lift

embassy Botschaft ① *bawt*·shaft

English Englisch ⓝ *eng*·lish
enough genug ge·*nook*
enter eintreten *ain*·tray·ten
evening Abend ⓜ *ah*·bent
everything alles *a*·les
exchange wechseln *vek*·seln
exhibition Ausstellung ⓕ
ows·shte·lung
exit Ausgang ⓜ *ows*·gang
expensive teuer *toy*·er
express mail Expresspost ⓕ
eks·*pres*·post

-f-

fall (autumn) Herbst ⓜ herpst
family Familie ⓕ fa·*mee*·li·e
fast schnell shnel
father Vater ⓜ *fah*·ter
fever Fieber ⓝ *fee*·ber
film (cinema/camera) Film ⓜ film
fine (payment) Geldbuße ⓕ
gelt·boo·se
finger Finger ⓜ *fing*·er
first class erste Klasse ⓕ *er*·ste
kla·se
fish shop Fischgeschäft ⓝ
fish·ge·sheft
flight Flug ⓜ flook
floor (storey) Stock ⓜ shtok
footpath Gehweg ⓜ *gay*·vayk
foreign ausländisch *ows*·len·dish
forest Wald ⓜ valt
free (gratis) gratis *grah*·tis
fresh (not stale) frisch frish
friend Freund(in) ⓜ/ⓕ froynt/
froyn·din

-g-

garden Garten ⓜ *gar*·ten
gas (for cooking) Gas ⓝ gahs
gas (petrol) Benzin ⓝ ben·*tseen*

gift Geschenk ⓝ ge·*shengk*
girl Mädchen ⓝ *mayt*·khen
girlfriend Freundin ⓕ *froyn*·din
glasses (spectacles) Brille ⓕ
bri·le
glove Handschuh ⓜ *hant*·shoo
go (by vehicle) fahren *fah*·ren
go (on foot) gehen *gay*·en
grocery store Lebensmittelladen ⓜ
lay·bens·mi·tel·lah·den
guided tour Führung ⓕ *fü*·rung

-h-

half Hälfte ⓕ *helf*·te
heater Heizgerät ⓝ *haits*·ge·rayt
help helfen *hel*·fen
here hier heer
hire mieten *mee*·ten
holidays Ferien pl *fair*·ri·en
honeymoon Flitterwochen ⓕ pl
fli·ter·vo·khen
hospital Krankenhaus ⓝ
krang·ken·hows
hot heiß hais
husband Ehemann ⓜ *ay*·e·man

-i-

identification Ausweis ⓜ *ows*·vais
identification card Personalausweis
ⓜ per·zo·*nahl*·ows·vais
ill krank krangk
included inbegriffen *in*·be·gri·fen
information Auskunft ⓕ *ows*·kunft
insurance Versicherung ⓕ
fer·*zi*·khe·rung
internet cafe Internetcafé ⓝ
in·ter·net·ka·fay
interpreter Dolmetscher(in) ⓜ/ⓕ
dol·met·sher/*dol*·met·she·rin
itinerary Reiseroute ⓕ *rai*·ze·roo·te

-j-

jacket Jacke ① *ya*·ke
jeans Jeans ① pl dzheens
jewellery Schmuck ⑩ shmuk
jumper (sweater) Pullover ⑩
pu·*law*·ver

-k-

key Schlüssel ⑩ *shlü*·sel
kind nett net
kitchen Küche ① *kü*·khe

-l-

large groß graws
last letzte *lets*·te
late spät shpayt
laundrette Wäscherei ① ve·she·*rai*
leather Leder ⑩ *lay*·der
left luggage Gepäckaufbewahrung ①
ge·*pek*·owf·be·vah·rung
letter (mail) Brief ⑩ breef
lift (elevator) Lift ⑩ lift
linen (bed) Bettwäsche ① *bet*·ve·she
locked abgeschlossen *ap*·ge·shlo·sen
lost verloren fer·*law*·ren
lost property office Fundbüro ⑩
funt·bü·raw
luggage Gepäck ⑩ ge·*pek*
luggage lockers Schließfächer ⑩ pl
shlees·fe·kher
lunch Mittagessen ⑩ *mi*·tahk·e·sen

-m-

mail Post ① post
make-up Schminke ① *shming*·ke
man Mann ⑩ man
manager Manager(in) ⑩/①
me·ne·*dzher*/me·ne·*dzhe*·rin

map Karte ① *kar*·te
market Markt ⑩ markt
meat Fleisch ⑩ flaish
medicine Medizin ① me·di·*tseen*
metro station U-Bahnhof ⑩
oo·bahn·hawf
midnight Mitternacht ① *mi*·ter·nakht
milk Milch ① milkh
mineral water Mineralwasser ⑩
mi·ne·*rahl*·va·ser
mobile phone Handy ⑩ *hen*·di
modem Modem ⑩ *maw*·dem
money Geld ⑩ gelt
month Monat ⑩ *maw*·nat
mother Mutter ① *mu*·ter
motorcycle Motorrad ⑩ *maw*·tor·raht
motorway (tollway) Autobahn ①
ow·to·bahn
mountain Berg ⑩ berk
museum Museum ⑩ mu·*zay*·um
music Musik ① mu·*zeek*

-n-

name Name ⑩ *nah*·me
napkin Serviette ① zer·*vye*·te
nappy (diaper) Windel ① *vin*·del
newsagency Zeitungshändler ⑩
tsai·tungks·hen·dler
newspaper Zeitung ① *tsai*·tung
next nächste *naykhs*·te
night Nacht ① nakht
no nein nain
nonsmoking nichtraucher
nikht·row·kher
now jetzt yetst
number Zahl ① tsahl

-o-

oil Öl ⑩ erl
open (not closed) offen *o*·fen

opening hours Öffnungszeiten ① pl
erf·nungks·tsai·ten
order bestellen *be·shte·len*

-p-

painter Maler(in) ⓜ/① *mah·ler/
mah·le·rin*
painting (the art) Malerei ①
mah·le·rai
pants (trousers) Hose ① *haw·ze*
pantyhose Strumpfhose ①
shtrumpf·haw·ze
paper Papier ⓝ *pa·peer*
party Fest ⓝ *fest*
passenger (bus/taxi) Fahrgast ⓜ
fahr·gast
passenger (plane) Fluggast ⓜ
flook·gast
passport (Reise)Pass ⓜ (*rai·ze·*)*pas*
path Pfad ⓜ *pfaht*
penknife Taschenmesser ⓝ
ta·shen·me·ser
pensioner Rentner(in) ⓜ/① *rent·ner/
rent·ne·rin*
petrol Benzin ⓝ *ben·tseen*
phone book Telefonbuch ⓝ
te·le·fawn·bookh
phonecard Telefonkarte ①
te·le·fawn·kar·te
phrasebook Sprachführer ⓜ
shprahkh·fü·rer
pillow Kissen ⓝ *ki·sen*
pillowcase Kissenbezug ⓜ
ki·sen·be·tsook
platform Bahnsteig ⓜ *bahn·shtaik*
play (theatre) Schauspiel ⓝ
show·shpeel
police Polizei ① *po·li·tsai*
police station Polizeirevier ⓝ
po·li·tsai·re·veer
post office Postamt ⓝ *post·amt*
postcard Postkarte ① *post·kar·te*
postcode Postleitzahl ① *post·lai·tsahl*

pound (money/weight) Pfund ⓝ
pfunt
present (gift) Geschenk ⓝ
ge·shengk
price Preis ⓜ *prais*

-q-

quick schnell *shnel*
quiet ruhig *roo·ikh*

-r-

receipt Quittung ① *kvi·tung*
refund Rückzahlung ①
rük·tsah·lung
rent mieten *mee·ten*
repair reparieren *re·pa·ree·ren*
return zurückkommen
tsu·rük·ko·men
return ticket Rückfahrkarte ①
rük·fahr·kar·te
road Straße ① *shtrah·se*
room Zimmer ⓝ *tsi·mer*
route Route ① *roo·te*

-s-

safe Safe ⓜ *sayf*
sea Meer ⓝ *mair*
season Jahreszeit ① *yah·res·tsait*
seat (car) Sitz ⓜ *zits*
seat (train/cinema) Platz ⓜ *plats*
seatbelt Sicherheitsgurt ⓜ
zi·kher·haits·gurt
service charge Bedienungszuschlag
ⓜ *be·dee·nungks·tsoo·shlahk*
share (with) teilen (mit) *tai·len (mit)*
shirt Hemd ⓝ *hemt*
shoes Schuhe ⓜ pl *shoo·e*
shop Geschäft ⓝ *ge·sheft*
shopping centre Einkaufszentrum ⓝ
ain·kowfs·tsen·trum

show zeigen *tsai*·gen
shower Dusche ⓕ *doo*·she
sick krank krangk
silk Seide ⓕ *zai*·de
silver silbern *zil*·bern
single (unmarried) ledig *lay*·dikh
single room Einzelzimmer ⓝ *ain*·tsel·tsi·mer
sister Schwester ⓕ *shves*·ter
size Größe ⓕ *grer*·se
skirt Rock ⓜ rok
sleeping bag Schlafsack ⓜ *shlahf*·zak
sleeping car Schlafwagen ⓜ *shlahf*·vah·gen
slide (film) Dia ⓝ *dee*·a
snack Snack ⓜ snek
snow Schnee ⓜ shnay
socks Socken ⓕ pl *zo*·ken
son Sohn ⓜ zawn
soon bald balt
spring (season) Frühling ⓜ *frü*·ling
square (town) Platz ⓜ plats
stairway Treppe ⓕ *tre*·pe
stamp Briefmarke ⓕ *breef*·mar·ke
stationer Schreibwarenhandlung ⓕ *shraip*·vah·ren·han·dlung
street Straße ⓕ *shtrah*·se
student Student(in) ⓜ/ⓕ shtu·*dent*/shtu·*den*·tin
subtitles Untertitel ⓜ pl *un*·ter·tee·tel
suitcase Koffer ⓜ *ko*·fer
summer Sommer ⓜ *zo*·mer
supermarket Supermarkt ⓜ *zoo*·per·markt
surface mail normale Post ⓕ nor·*mah*·le post
surname Nachname ⓜ *nahkh*·nah·me
sweater Pullover ⓜ pu·*law*·ver
swim schwimmen *shvi*·men
swimming pool Schwimmbad ⓝ *shvim*·baht

- t -

taxi stand Taxistand ⓜ *tak*·si·shtant
ticket (bus/metro/train) Fahrkarte ⓕ *fahr*·kar·te
ticket (cinema/museum) Eintrittskarte ⓕ *ain*·trits·kar·te
ticket (plane) Flugticket ⓝ *flook*·ti·ket
ticket machine Fahrkartenautomat ⓜ *fahr*·kar·ten·ow·to·maht
ticket office Fahrkartenverkauf ⓜ *fahr*·kar·ten·fer·kowf
ticket office (theatre) Theaterkasse ⓕ te·*ah*·ter·ka·se
time Zeit ⓕ tsait
timetable Fahrplan ⓜ *fahr*·plahn
tip (gratuity) Trinkgeld ⓝ *tringk*·gelt
today heute *hoy*·te
tomorrow morgen *mor*·gen
tour Tour ⓕ toor
tourist office Fremdenverkehrsbüro ⓝ *frem*·den·fer·kairs·bü·raw
town Stadt ⓕ shtat
train station Bahnhof ⓜ *bahn*·hawf
transit lounge Transitraum ⓜ tran·*zeet*·rowm
travel agency Reisebüro ⓝ *rai*·ze·bü·raw
travellers cheque Reisescheck ⓜ *rai*·ze·shek
trip Reise ⓕ *rai*·ze
trousers Hose ⓕ *haw*·ze
twin beds zwei Einzelbetten ⓝ pl tsvai *ain*·tsel·be·ten

- u -

underwear Unterwäsche ⓕ *un*·ter·ve·she
urgent dringend *dring*·ent

~ v ~

vacant frei frai
vacation Ferien pl *fair·i·en*
validate (ticket) entwerten ent·*ver*·ten
vegetable Gemüse ⓝ ge·*mü*·ze
view Aussicht ① *ows*·zikht

~ w ~

waiting room (doctor's)
Wartezimmer ⓝ *var*·te·tsi·mer
waiting room (train station)
Wartesaal ⓜ *var*·te·zahl
walk gehen *gay*·en
warm warm varm
wash (oneself) sich waschen zikh
va·shen
washing machine Waschmaschine ①
vash·ma·shee·ne

watch Uhr ① oor
water Wasser ⓝ *va*·ser
weekend Wochenende ⓝ
vo·khen·en·de
when wann van
where wo vaw
who wer vair
wife Ehefrau ① *ay*·e·frow
window Fenster ⓝ *fens*·ter
wine Wein ⓜ vain
woman Frau ① frow
wool Wolle ① *vo*·le

~ y ~

year Jahr ⓝ yahr
yesterday gestern *ges*·tern
youth hostel Jugendherberge ①
yoo·gent·her·ber·ge

Dictionary

GERMAN *to* ENGLISH

deutsch – englisch

Nouns in this dictionary, and adjectives affected by gender, have their gender indicated by ⓕ, ⓜ or ⓝ. If it's a plural noun, you'll also see pl. Where a word that could be either a noun or a verb has no gender indicated, it's a verb.

~ a ~

Abend ⓜ *ah*·bent evening
Abendessen ⓝ *ah*·bent·e·sen dinner
abfahren *ap*·fah·ren leave (depart)
Abfahrt ⓕ *ap*·fahrt departure
abgeschlossen *ap*·ge·shlo·sen locked
alkoholfreies Getränk ⓝ al·ko·*hawl*·frai·es ge·*trengk* soft drink
alle *a*·le all
Allee ⓕ a·*lay* avenue
allein a·*lain* alone
alles *a*·les everything
alltäglich al·*tayk*·likh every day
alt alt old • ancient
an an at • to
andere *an*·de·re other • different

ankommen *an*·ko·men arrive
Ankunft ⓕ *an*·kunft arrivals
Anzahlung ⓕ *an*·tsah·lung deposit
Apotheke ⓕ a·po·*tay*·ke chemist • pharmacy
Arzt ⓜ artst doctor (medical)
Ärztin ⓕ *erts*·tin doctor (medical)
auch owkh too • also
auf owf on • at
Auge ⓝ *ow*·ge eye
Augenblick ⓜ *ow*·gen·blik moment
aus ows from • out
Ausgang ⓜ *ows*·gang exit
ausgebucht ows·ge·bookht booked out
Auskunft ⓕ *ows*·kunft information
Aussicht ⓕ *ows*·zikht view
Aussichtspunkt ⓜ ows·zikhts·pungkt lookout

82

Ausstellung ⓕ *ows*·shte·lung exhibition
ausverkauft ows·fer·kowft sold out
Ausweis ⓜ *ows*·vais identification
Auto ⓝ *ow*·to car
Autobahn ⓕ *ow*·to·bahn motorway (tollway)
automatisch ow·to·*mah*·tish automatic
Autoverleih ⓜ *ow*·to·fer·lai car hire

- b -

Bad ⓝ baht bath
Badeanzug ⓜ *bah*·de·an·tsook swimsuit
Badezimmer ⓝ *bah*·de·tsi·mer bathroom
Bahnhof ⓜ *bahn*·hawf railway station
Bahnsteig ⓜ *bahn*·shtaik platform
Bankkonto ⓝ *bangk*·kon·to bank account
Bargeld ⓝ *bahr*·gelt cash
Batterie ⓕ ba·te·*ree* battery
Baumwolle ⓕ *bowm*·vo·le cotton
Bedienungszuschlag ⓜ be·*dee*·nungks·tsoo·shlahk service charge
Benzin ⓝ ben·*tseen* gas/petrol
Beruf ⓜ be·*roof* occupation • profession
berühren be·*rü*·ren touch
besser *be*·ser better
beste *bes*·te best
besteigen be·*shtai*·gen board (plane, ship)
bestellen be·*shte*·len order
Bestellung ⓕ be·*shte*·lung order (restaurant)
besuchen be·*zoo*·khen visit
Betrag ⓜ be·*trahk* amount
Bett ⓝ bet bed
Bettlaken ⓝ *bet*·lah·ken sheet (bed)
Bettzeug ⓝ *bet*·tsoyk bedding
bezahlen be·*tsah*·len pay
Bier ⓝ beer beer

billig *bi*·likh cheap
bitte *bi*·te please
bleiben *blai*·ben stay (remain)
Boot ⓝ bawt boat
(an) Bord an bort aboard
Botschaft ⓕ *bawt*·shaft embassy
Briefmarke ⓕ *breef*·mar·ke stamp
Brot ⓝ brawt bread
Bruder ⓜ *broo*·der brother
Buch ⓝ bookh book
buchen *boo*·khen book (reserve)
Buchhandlung ⓕ *bookh*·han·dlung bookshop
Burg ⓕ burk castle
Busbahnhof ⓜ *bus*·bahn·hawf bus station
Bushaltestelle ⓕ *bus*·hal·te·shte·le bus stop

- d -

Dämmerung ⓕ *de*·me·rung dawn • dusk
danken *dang*·ken thank
Datum ⓝ *dah*·tum date (day)
dein dain your sg inf
Denkmal ⓝ *dengk*·mahl monument
Deutsch ⓝ doytsh German
Dienstag ⓜ *deens*·tahk Tuesday
Dolmetscher(in) ⓜ/ⓕ *dol*·met·sher/ *dol*·met·she·rin interpreter
Dom ⓜ dawm cathedral
Donnerstag ⓜ *do*·ners·tahk Thursday
Doppelbett ⓝ *do*·pel·bet double bed
Doppelzimmer ⓝ *do*·pel·tsi·mer double room
Dorf ⓝ dorf village
dort dort there
Dosenöffner ⓜ *daw*·zen·erf·ner can opener
draußen *drow*·sen outside
du doo you sg inf
dünn dün thin

durch durkh through
Dusche ① doo·she shower

- e -

Ecke ① e·ke corner
Ehe ① ay·e marriage
Ehefrau ① ay·e·frow wife
Ehemann ⓜ ay·e·man husband
Ei ⓝ ai egg
ein(s) ain(s) one
einfach ain·fakh simple
einfache Fahrkarte ① ain·fa·khe
fahr·kar·te one-way ticket
einige ai·ni·ge some • several
einmal ain·mahl once
eintreten ain·tray·ten enter
Eintrittsgeld ⓝ ain·trits·gelt
cover charge
Eintrittskarte ⓜ ain·trits·kar·te
(admission) ticket
Eintrittspreis ⓜ ain·trits·prais
admission price
Einzelzimmer ⓝ ain·tsel·tsi·mer
single room
Eis ⓝ ais ice
Eiscreme ① ais·kraym ice cream
Endstation ① ent·shta·tsyawn
terminal
entwerten ent·ver·ten validate
(ticket)
er air he
Erdnuss ① ert·nus peanut •
ground nut
erste ers·te first
Erwachsene ⓜ&① er·vak·se·ne
adult
Essen ⓝ e·sen food
essen e·sen eat
etwas et·vas something • anything

- f -

fahren fah·ren travel by vehicle
Fahrgast ⓜ fahr·gast passenger

(bus/taxi)
Fahrkarte ① fahr·kar·te ticket
Fahrkartenverkauf ⓜ
fahr·kar·ten·fer·kowf ticket office
Fahrplan ⓜ fahr·plahn timetable
Fahrrad ⓝ fahr·raht bicycle
Fahrzeugpapiere ⓝ pl
fahr·tsoyk·pa·pee·re car owner's title
(document)
Familienname ⓜ fa·mee·li·en·nah·me
family name
Familienstand ⓜ fa·mee·li·en·shtant
marital status
Fenster ⓝ fens·ter window
Ferien pl fair·ri·en holidays •
vacation
Fernbus ⓜ fern·bus bus (intercity)
Fernseher ⓜ fern·zay·er TV set
fertig fer·tikh ready • finished
Fest ⓝ fest festival • party
Flasche ① fla·she bottle
Flaschenöffner ⓜ fla·shen·erf·ner
bottle opener
Fleisch ⓝ flaish meat
fliegen flee·gen fly
Flug ⓜ flook flight
Flughafen ⓜ flook·hah·fen airport
Flugticket ⓝ flook·ti·ket plane ticket
Flugzeug ⓝ flook·tsoyk aeroplane
Frankreich ⓝ frangk·raikh France
Frau ① frow wife • woman
frei frai free (not bound) • vacant
Freitag ⓜ frai·tahk Friday
Fremdenverkehrsbüro ⓝ
frem·den·fer·kairs·bü·raw tourist office
frisch frish fresh (not stale)
Friseur(in) ⓜ/① fri·zer/fri·zer·rin
hairdresser
Frühstück ⓝ frü·shtük breakfast
Führerschein ⓜ fü·rer·shain driving
licence
Führung ① fü·rung guided tour
Fußball ⓜ foos·bal football • soccer
Fußgänger(in) ⓜ/① foos·geng·er/
foos·geng·e·rin pedestrian

-g-

Garderobe ① gar·draw·be wardrobe • cloakroom
Gebäude ⑩ ge·boy·de building
Geburtsdatum ⑩ ge·burts·dah·tum date of birth
Geburtsort ⑩ ge·burts·ort place of birth
Geburtstag ⑩ ge·burts·tahk birthday
gefährlich ge·fair·likh dangerous
gehen gay·en walk
Gehweg ⑩ gay·vayk footpath
Geld ⑩ gelt money
Geldautomat ⑩ gelt·ow·to·maht automatic teller machine (ATM)
Geldwechsel ⑩ gelt·vek·sel currency exchange
genug ge·nook enough
Gepäck ⑩ ge·pek luggage
Gepäckaufbewahrung ①
ge·pek·owf·be·vah·rung left luggage
gerade ge·rah·de straight (direction)
Geschäft ⑩ ge·sheft shop • business
Geschenk ⑩ ge·shengk present (gift)
geschlossen ge·shlo·sen closed
gestern ges·tern yesterday
Getränk ⑩ ge·trengk drink (beverage)
Gewicht ⑩ ge·vikht weight
Gleis ⑩ glais platform
groß graws big • great • tall
Größe ① grer·se size (general)
grün grün green
gut goot good • well

-h-

Haar ⑩ hahr hair
haben hah·ben have
Hälfte ① helf·te half
Halskette ① hals·ke·te necklace
Halt ⑩ halt stop
handgemacht hant·ge·makht handmade
Handtasche ① hant·ta·she handbag

Handwerk ⑩ hant·verk crafts
Handy ⑩ hen·di mobile phone
Hauptplatz ⑩ howpt·plats main square
heiß hais hot
Heizgerät ⑩ haits·ge·rayt heater
helfen hel·fen help
hell hel light (weight)
heute hoy·te today
hier heer here
Hilfe ① hil·fe help
hinten hin·ten at the back
hinter hin·ter behind
hinüber hi·nü·ber across (to)
hoch hawkh high (up)
Hochzeit ① hokh·tsait wedding
Höhle ① her·le cave
Holz ⑩ holts wood
Honig ⑩ haw·nikh honey
hören her·ren hear • listen

-i-

inbegriffen in·be·gri·fen included
innen i·nen inside
Innenstadt ① i·nen·shtat city centre
Insel ① in·zel island
irgendein ir·gent·ain any
irgendetwas ir·gent·et·vas anything
irgendwo ir·gent·vaw anywhere

-j-

ja yah yes
Jahr ⑩ yahr year
jeder ⑩ yay·der each • every
jemand yay·mant someone
jetzt yetst now
Jugendherberge ①
yoo·gent·her·ber·ge youth hostel
jung yung young
Junge ⑩ yung·e boy

-k-

Kaffee ⑩ ka·fay coffee
kalt kalt cold

kaputt ka·*put* broken
Karte ① *kar*·te map • ticket
Kasse ① *ka*·se cash register •
checkout • ticket counter
kaufen *kow*·fen buy
keine *kai*·ne none
Kellner(in) ⓜ/① *kel*·ner/*kel*·ne·rin
waiter
kennen *ke*·nen know (a person)
Kinder ⓝ pl *kin*·der children
Kino ⓝ *kee*·no cinema
Kiosk ⓜ *kee*·osk convenience
store
Kirche ① *kir*·khe church
Kissen ⓝ *ki*·sen pillow
Kleidung ① *klai*·dung clothing
klein klain little • small• short
(height)
Kleingeld ⓝ *klain*·gelt loose change
Klimaanlage ① *klee*·ma·an·lah·ge
air-conditioning
Kloster ⓝ *klaws*·ter convent •
monastery
Kneipe ① *knai*·pe pub
Knopf ⓜ *knopf* button
Koch ⓜ kokh chef • cook
kochen *ko*·khen cook
Koffer ⓜ *ko*·fer suitcase
Kofferraum ⓜ *ko*·fer·rowm boot •
trunk
kommen *ko*·men come
Konditorei ① kon·dee·to·*rai*
cake shop
können *ker*·nen be able to • have
permission to
Kontaktlinsen ① pl kon·*takt*·lin·zen
contact lenses
Kopf ⓜ kopf head
kosten *kos*·ten cost
krank krangk sick
Krankenhaus ⓝ *krang*·ken·hows
hospital
Krankenpfleger ⓜ
krang·ken·pflay·ger nurse
Krankenschwester ①
krang·ken·shves·ter nurse

Krankenwagen ⓜ *krang*·ken·vah·gen
ambulance
Küche ① *kü*·khe kitchen
Kühlschrank ⓜ *kül*·shrangk
refrigerator
Kunst ① kunst art
Kunstgalerie ① *kunst*·ga·le·ree
art gallery
Kunstgewerbe ⓝ *kunst*·ge·ver·be
arts & crafts
Kunsthandwerk ⓝ *kunst*·hant·verk
handicrafts
Künstler(in) ⓜ/① *künst*·ler/
künst·le·rin artist
Kunstwerk ⓝ *kunst*·verk work of art
kurz kurts short
Küste ① *küs*·te coast

-*l*-

Land ⓝ lant country • countryside
Landschaft ① *lant*·shaft scenery
lang lang long
langsam *lang*·zahm slow • slowly
laufen *low*·fen run
laut lowt loud • noisy
Lebensmittelladen ⓜ
lay·bens·mi·tel·lah·den grocery store
Leder ⓝ *lay*·der leather
leer lair empty
leicht laikht easy
leihen *lai*·en borrow
Lesbierin ① *les*·bi·e·rin lesbian
lesen *lay*·zen read
letzte *lets*·te last
Licht ⓝ likht light
Lift ⓜ lift lift • elevator
links lingks left (direction)
Lokal ⓝ lo·*kahl* bar
Luftpost ① *luft*·post airmail
luxuriös luk·su·ri·*ers* luxury

-*m*-

Mädchen ⓝ *mayt*·khen girl
Mann ⓜ man husband • man
Mantel ⓜ *man*·tel overcoat • cloak

Markt ⓜ markt market
Marktplatz ⓜ markt·plats market
square
Maschine ⓕ ma·shee·ne machine
Meer ⓝ mair sea
mehr mair more
mein main mine • my
mieten mee·ten rent • hire
Mikrowelle ⓕ mee·kro·ve·le
microwave
Milch ⓕ milkh milk
Mineralwasser ⓝ mi·ne·rahl·va·ser
mineral water
mit mit with
Mittag ⓜ mi·tahk noon
Mittagessen ⓝ mi·tahk·e·sen lunch
Mitteilung ⓕ mi·tai·lung message
Mitternacht ⓕ mi·ter·nakht midnight
Mittwoch ⓜ mit·vokh Wednesday
mögen mer·gen to like
möglich merk·likh possible
Monat ⓜ maw·nat month
Montag ⓜ mawn·tahk Monday
Morgen ⓜ mor·gen morning
morgen mor·gen tomorrow
Motorrad ⓝ maw·tor·raht
motorcycle
Münzen ⓕ pl mün·tsen coins
Mutter ⓕ mu·ter mother

- n -

nach nahkh after • towards
Nachmittag ⓜ nahkh·mi·tahk
afternoon
Nachname ⓜ nahkh·nah·me
surname
Nachrichten pl nahkh·rikh·ten
news
nächste naykhs·te next • nearest
Nacht ⓕ nakht night
nehmen nay·men take
nein nain no
neu noy new
nicht nikht not
nichtraucher nikht·row·kher

non-smoking
nichts nikhts nothing
nie nee never
Norden ⓜ nor·den north
normale Post ⓕ nor·mah·le post
surface mail
Notfall ⓜ nawt·fal emergency
Notizbuch ⓝ no·teets·bookh
notebook
Nummer ⓕ nu·mer number
nur noor only
Nuss ⓕ nus nut

- o -

Objektiv ⓝ op·yek·teef lens
(camera)
oder aw·der or
Ofen ⓜ aw·fen oven
offen o·fen open
öffnen erf·nen open
Öffnungszeiten ⓕ pl
erf·nungks·tsai·ten opening hours
oft oft often
ohne aw·ne without
örtlich ert·likh local
Osten ⓜ os·ten east
Ostern ⓝ aws·tern Easter
Österreich ⓝ ers·ter·raikh
Austria

- p -

Parkplatz ⓜ park·plats carpark
Pass ⓜ pas pass • passport
Pension ⓕ pahng·zyawn boarding
house • bed & breakfast
Personalausweis ⓜ
per·zo·nahl·ows·vais identification card
Pfad ⓜ pfaht path • trail
Pfund ⓝ pfunt pound (weight)
Polizei ⓕ po·li·tsai police
Polizeirevier ⓝ po·li·tsai·re·veer
police station
Postamt ⓝ post·amt post office
Postleitzahl ⓕ post·lai·tsahl
postcode

87

Preis ⓜ prais price
privat pri·*vaht* private
pro praw per

- q -

Quittung ⓕ *kvi*·tung receipt

- r -

Rabatt ⓜ ra·*bat* discount
radfahren *raht*·fah·ren cycle
Rasierer ⓜ ra·*zee*·rer razor
rauchen *row*·khen smoke
Rechnung ⓕ *rekh*·nung bill • check
rechts rekhts right (direction)
Reinigung ⓕ *rai*·ni·gung cleaning
Reise ⓕ *rai*·ze journey • trip
Reisebüro ⓝ *rai*·ze·bü·raw travel agency
Reiseführer ⓜ *rai*·ze·fü·rer guidebook
reisen *rai*·zen travel
Reisepass ⓜ *rai*·ze·pas passport
Reiseroute ⓕ *rai*·ze·roo·te itinerary
Reiseziel ⓝ *rai*·ze·tseel destination
Rentner(in) ⓜ/ⓕ *rent*·ner/*rent*·ne·rin pensioner
Reservierung ⓕ re·zer·*vee*·rung reservation
R-Gespräch ⓝ *air*·ge·shpraykh collect call • reverse-charge call
richtig *rikh*·tikh right (correct)
Rückfahrkarte ⓕ *rük*·fahr·kar·te return (ticket)
Rückzahlung ⓕ *rük*·tsah·lung refund
ruhig *roo*·ikh quiet
rund runt round

- s -

Saft ⓜ zaft juice
Samstag ⓜ *zams*·tahk Saturday
sauber *zow*·ber clean
Scheck ⓜ shek cheque (bank)
schieben *shee*·ben push
schlafen *shlah*·fen sleep
Schlafsack ⓜ *shlahf*·zak sleeping bag

Schlafzimmer ⓝ *shlahf*·tsi·mer bedroom
schließen *shlee*·sen close (shut)
Schloss ⓝ shlos lock • palace
Schlüssel ⓜ *shlü*·sel key
Schminke ⓕ *shming*·ke make-up
Schmuck ⓜ shmuk jewellery
Schnee ⓜ shnay snow
schnell shnel quick
schon shawn yet • already
schön shern beautiful
schreiben *shrai*·ben write
Schweiz ⓕ shvaits Switzerland
schwer shvair difficult (task) • heavy
Schwimmbad ⓝ *shvim*·baht swimming pool
schwimmen *shvi*·men swim
See ⓜ zay lake
sehen *zay*·en see • look
sehr zair very
Seide ⓕ *zai*·de silk
Seife ⓕ *zai*·fe soap
Selbstbedienung ⓕ *zelpst*·be·dee·nung self-service
sicher *zi*·kher safe
Sicherheit ⓕ *zi*·kher·hait safety
Sie zee you sg pol & pl
Single ⓜ singl single (of person)
sitzen *zi*·tsen sit
skifahren *shee*·fah·ren ski
sofort zo·*fort* immediately
Sonnenaufgang ⓜ *zo*·nen·owf·gang sunrise
Sonnenbrille ⓕ *zo*·nen·bri·le sunglasses
Sonnencreme ⓕ *zo*·nen·kraym sunblock
Sonnenuntergang ⓜ *zo*·nen·un·ter·gang sunset
Sonntag ⓜ *zon*·tahk Sunday
Speisekarte ⓕ *shpai*·ze·kar·te menu
Sprachführer ⓜ *shprahkh*·fü·rer phrasebook
sprechen *shpre*·khen speak
Stadt ⓕ shtat city • town
Stiefel ⓜ *shtee*·fel boot (footwear)

Stock ⓜ shtok floor (storey)
stornieren shtor·nee·ren cancel
Strand ⓜ shtrant beach
Straße ⓕ shtrah·se street • road
Straßenbahn ⓕ shtrah·sen·bahn tram
Straßenkarte ⓕ shtrah·sen·kar·te road map
Stück ⓝ shtük piece
Studentenausweis ⓜ shtu·den·ten·ows·vais student card
Stufe ⓕ shtoo·fe step (stairs)
Stuhl ⓜ shtool chair
Sturm ⓜ shturm storm
Süden ⓜ zü·den south

- t -

Tag ⓜ tahk day
täglich tayk·likh daily
Tasche ⓕ ta·she bag • pocket
Tee ⓜ tay tea
telefonieren te·le·fo·nee·ren phone
Telefonkarte ⓕ te·le·fawn·kar·te phone card
Telefonzelle ⓕ te·le·fawn·tse·le phone box
teuer toy·er expensive
Theaterkasse ⓕ te·ah·ter·ka·se ticket office (theatre)
Toilette ⓕ to·a·le·te toilet
Touristenklasse ⓕ tu·ris·ten·kla·se economy class
trinken tring·ken drink
Trinkgeld ⓝ tringk·gelt tip (gratuity)
trocken tro·ken dry
tun toon do
Tür ⓕ tür door
Turm ⓜ turm tower

- u -

U-Bahn ⓕ oo·bahn subway (underground)
U-Bahnhof ⓜ oo·bahn·hawf metro station

über ü·ber about • above • over
übermorgen ü·ber·mor·gen day after tomorrow
übernachten ü·ber·nakh·ten stay (at a hotel)
übersetzen ü·ber·ze·tsen translate
Uhr ⓕ oor clock • watch
umsteigen um·shtai·gen change (trains)
unmöglich un·merk·likh impossible
unter un·ter among • below • under
Unterkunft ⓕ un·ter·kunft accommodation
Unterschrift ⓕ un·ter·shrift signature
Untertitel ⓜ pl un·ter·tee·tel subtitles

- v -

Verbindung ⓕ fer·bin·dung connection
Versicherung ⓕ fer·zi·khe·rung insurance
Verspätung ⓕ fer·shpay·tung delay
viele fee·le many
vielleicht fi·laikht maybe
Visum ⓝ vee·zum visa
voll fol full
von fon from
vor fawr in front of • before
Vormittag ⓜ fawr·mi·tahk morning
Vorname ⓜ fawr·nah·me given name

- w -

Wagen ⓜ vah·gen carriage (train)
Wald ⓜ valt forest
wandern van·dern hike
wann van when
warten var·ten wait
warum va·rum why
was vas what
waschen va·shen wash (something)
Wäscherei ⓕ ve·she·rai laundrette
Wasser ⓝ va·ser water
wasserdicht va·ser·dikht waterproof
Wasserfall ⓜ va·ser·fal waterfall

Wasserflasche ① *va·ser·fla·she* water bottle
Wasserhahn ⓜ *va·ser·hahn* tap
Wechselgeld ⑩ *vek·sel·gelt* change (coins)
Wechselkurs ⓜ *vek·sel·kurs* exchange rate
wechseln *vek·seln* exchange (money)
Wecker ⓜ *ve·ker* alarm clock
Weg ⓜ *vayk* track (path) • way
wegen *vay·gen* because of
weil *vail* because
Wein ⓜ *vain* wine
Weinberg ⓜ *vain·berk* vineyard
weiß *vais* white
weit *vait* far
wenig *vay·nikh* (a) little
wenige *vay·ni·ge* few
weniger *vay·ni·ger* less
wenn *ven* when • if
wer *vair* who
Wert ⓜ *vert* value (price)
Westen ⓜ *ves·ten* west
Wetter ⑩ *ve·ter* weather
wichtig *vikh·tikh* important
wie *vee* how
wie viel *vee feel* how much
wieder *vee·der* again
wiegen *vee·gen* weigh
willkommen *vil·ko·men* welcome
windig *vin·dikh* windy
wir *veer* we
wissen *vi·sen* know (something)
wo *vaw* where
Wochenende ⑩ *vo·khen·en·de* weekend
Wohnung ① *vaw·nung* apartment (flat)
Wohnwagen ⓜ *vawn·vah·gen* caravan
Wolke ① *vol·ke* cloud
Wolle ① *vo·le* wool
wollen *vo·len* want
Wort ⑩ *vort* word
Wörterbuch ⑩ *ver·ter·bookh* dictionary

wunderbar *vun·der·bahr* wonderful
wünschen *vün·shen* wish

~ Z ~

Zahl ① *tsahl* number
Zahlung ① *tsah·lung* payment
Zahnarzt ⓜ *tsahn·artst* dentist
Zahnärztin ① *tsahn·erts·tin* dentist
Zahnpasta ① *tsahn·pas·ta* toothpaste
zeigen *tsai·gen* show • point
Zeit ① *tsait* time
Zeitschrift ① *tsait·shrift* magazine
Zeitung ① *tsai·tung* newspaper
Zeitungshändler ⓜ *tsai·tungks·hen·dler* newsagency
Zeitungskiosk ⓜ *tsai·tungks·kee·osk* newsstand
Zeitunterschied ⓜ *tsait·un·ter·sheet* time difference
Zelt ⑩ *tselt* tent
zelten *tsel·ten* camp
Zeltplatz ⓜ *tselt·plats* campsite
Zentimeter ⓜ *tsen·ti·may·ter* centimetre
Zentralheizung ①
tsen·trahl·hai·tsung central heating
Zentrum ⑩ *tsen·trum* centre
zerbrechen *tser·bre·khen* break
zerbrechlich *tser·brekh·likh* fragile
ziehen *tsee·en* pull
Zimmer ⑩ *tsi·mer* room
Zimmernummer ① *tsi·mer·nu·mer* room number
Zoll ⓜ *tsol* customs
zu *tsoo* too • at
Zug ⓜ *tsook* train
zurück *tsu·rük* back (return)
zurückkommen *tsu·rük·ko·men* return
zusammen *tsu·za·men* together
zweimal *tsvai·mahl* twice
zweite *tsvai·te* second
zwischen *tsvi·shen* between

Index